GUILLERMO GARCIA RODILES

FROM WAR

TO

Rock 'N Roll

A man's journey from a child in the
guerrilla war in Cuba to the greatest
Rock 'n Roll bands in the world.

From War to Rock 'N Roll

This is a nonfiction novel based on a true story and historical facts.

Published in the United States of America
Cover design by: Giorgio Sferra
Edited by: Natalie Rodiles, Rosita Rodiles, and Victor Nickolich.

From War to Rock 'N Roll—Garcia Rodiles, Guillermo —Ed. I. Title
1. Biography & Autobiography / Personal Memoirs
2. Biography & Autobiography / Political
3. History / Cuba-20th Century First Edition

To my dear mother, Antonia Rodiles.

From War to Rock 'n Roll

CONTENTS

I.   Author's Preface

II.   Introduction

III.   Part 1. ---- Castro's revolution – 1952 to 1959

1.   My Introduction to the Revolution

2.   Deliveries to the Rebels in the Mountains

3.   In the Mountains with the Rebels

IV.   Part 2. – Construction of Cuba's Socialist Republic

1.   Creation of Cuba's New Government

2.   Bay of Pigs invasion and the Cuban Missile Crisis

3.   My Enlistment in the Cuban Army

4.   Traveling with the Merchant Marine Corps

5.   My Escape from Cuba

V.   Part 3. – Guillermo, living in the United States

1.   My Arrival to the United States

From War to Rock 'n Roll

AUTHOR'S PREFACE

This book deals with my life in Cuba before and after the revolution of 1959, a revolution that placed Fidel Castro Ruz as the absolute ruler of the island until his death in 2016. It tells of my activities and personal life experiences as a young combatant during the war, a war that deprived me of my childhood.

Part One covers Castro's armed revolution aimed to end Batista's dictatorship and take over the government of the island. The second part reveals how the socialist republic, built by the people under the dictates of Fidel Castro, came to be. The last part of this book deals my escape from Cuba and my exciting and extraordinary life as a musician in the United States.

I was introduced to politics in Cuba when I was only eight years old. My whole family was deeply engaged with the revolution and had committed themselves to bring Batista's dictatorial regime to an end. I was greatly influenced by my family's convictions that their struggle would benefit the people of the island and thus I got involved in the rebel movement.

My first activities during the was making deliveries with my mother to the rebels in the mountains. She was responsible for running ammunition, medicines, bandages, and anything that she could procure for the rebel forces. I eventually joined my father in the mountains, who had been deployed with a guerilla detachment in a area known as Baracoa.

After the revolution's victory, I volunteered to serve in Castro's regular army. However, three years later I became very disillusioned with the strict military life and the loss of personal freedoms. I had wanted to become a pilot in the Cuban Air Force but, was rejected because of my poor disciplinary record during my time in the army. It was at that point in my life when I decided to make music my career.

At the time, professional music was almost inexistent in Cuba and I knew that I would have to leave the island to achieve that goal. I eventually managed to join the merchant marine corps and started travelling out of Cuba with the sole goal in mind to escape to freedom while at a foreign seaport.

From War to Rock 'n Roll is the story of my improbable journey from growing up as a child of war to a successful musician with some of the top rock performers in the United States.

INTRODUCTION

The island of Cuba was first inhabited by a handful of Indian tribes who lived under a primitive communal system. The Siboneyes, Guanahatabeyes and Tainos traded in goods rather than using a monetary system and there was no class distinction in their societies. In 1492, Christopher Columbus claimed control of the island under the name of the queen Isabel of Spain. The Spanish first named it "Juana", after the royal princess of Spain. Shortly thereafter they changed the name to "Ave Maria", ave meaning bird in Spanish. Then again, the name was changed to "Cuba", the meaning of which is still unknown to this day. Don Diego Velasquez, another Spaniard, founded the first city of the island and named it Baracoa. He also attempted to take a census of the population of the island's inhabitants, a difficult task due to the Indians' highly mobile lifestyle. His findings revealed there were approximately forty-thousand Indians living in Cuba.

Queen Isabella of Spain sent missionaries to the island to attempt to convert the Indians to Christianity but failed because the Indians refused to pray to any Gods other than their own. When Spain imported the cultivation of sugar cane in Cuba, the Indians were forced to work in the fields and many of them died as a result. Many succumbed to epidemics of small pox, rare diseases and to interracial marriages. When some of the Indians refused to work, the Spaniards set an example by burning alive a leader of one of the Indian tribes, a chief named Hatuey. In the end, the Indians turned out to be poor laborers who got sick very easy. To replace the dwindling Indian labor force, the Spaniards started importing slaves from Africa, a time that marked the beginning of the slave trade on the island.

In the years that followed, Spain kept control over Cuba with a large mercenary army, appointed all the island's officials and took all the profits from the island's sugar, tobacco, and fruit crops. Cuba had become a Spanish colony with a system of black slavery and a nearly extinct native population. The Spaniards went on to build forts throughout the island to use them for their defense against a possible foreign invasion.

By then, Cuba had already become a strategically important country for trade, particularly to England. In 1741, England invaded and took control of Cuba, but the harassment they faced from the guerrillas and the rare tropical diseases suffered by their troops made them give the island back to Spain a few months later.

In 1819, the island witnessed the first uprising by Cuban nationals against the Spanish colonial rule. All the rebels who took part in that insurrection were either killed in combat or executed by the Spanish soldiers at the end of the battle. More rebellions took place in 1826, 1828, and 1830 in 1848, 1851, and 1855 in protest of the Spanish colonial rule - the Cubans were constantly trying to gain their independence.

In 1868, Cuba witnessed a significant revolt involving negroes, mulattos and others who were opposed to the black slavery system. This time, a rich property owner, Carlos Manuel De Cespedes decided to free all his slaves in support of the revolt. Soon thereafter, Cespedes would become the president of the Cuban republic.

In 1878, the island went through a devastating war known as the *Ten-Year War* that cost the lives of many Spanish soldiers and Cuban rebels. In 1886, the Spanish government was forced to abolish slavery on the island and promised many other reforms for the benefit of the people. Those reforms became just another unfulfilled promise as Cuba continued to pour a stream of wealth into the Spanish economy while its own economy remained stagnant.

From War to Rock 'n Roll

The revolt against slavery on the island was carried out mostly by blacks,
mulatos, and others who believed
that slavery was wrong.
Maximo Gomez helped a great deal in the
battle against slavery. Carlos Manuel De Cespedes, a rich property owner at
the time, set all his slaves free in support of the cause.

Jose Marti was a Cuban who went into exile because of his subversive poetry writings against the government of Cuba. Jose Marti traveled half the world and collected money for different Cuban groups by selling his writings.

***

On May 19, 1895, the rebels set into action another revolt against the Spanish rule. A Cuban thinker and patriot named Jose Marti was killed in that battle, shot in the back while drinking water from a river. Despite the death, other men such as Antonio Maceo and Maximo Gomez kept the rebels organized to fight.

USS Maine, entering the Bay of Havana

In 1896 an American battleship, the USS Maine, arrived at bay of Habana to protect the American citizens on the island. On February fifteenth, 1898, the USS Maine exploded killing its entire crew of over one hundred men.

U.S. President McKinley blamed the sabotage on the Spaniards and declared war on Spain on April 21st, 1898. The U.S. won this war. In payment for the lives of the men lost on the "Maine", the United States took from Spain the Philippines Islands, Puerto Rico and Guam. The Spanish left Cuba on 10th, 1898 and a treaty was then signed between the United States government and the Cuban government. The treaty gave the United States authority to begin what was to be known as *The*

Pacification Program of Cuba. Soon thereafter, the United States sent their troops to Cuba, including regiments of engineers and infantrymen.

In 1901, the United States senate wrote and approved an amendment called the "Platt Amendment", which gave the U.S. government the right to intervene in the democratic system that has been established on the island, and to protect Cuba.

Jose Marti, a Cuban exiled for his subversive poetry writings against the Spanish government, went on to travel around the world to organize other Cuban exiles and raise money for the cause by selling his writings. It was around that time that the "Platt Amendment" was sent to Cuba for approval. By then, many American soldiers were already deployed in Cuba with the intention to remain until the amendment was signed.

The amendment stipulated that the United States government would have the authority to intervene in Cuba's internal affairs at any time to protect the independence of Cuba. It also stipulated that Cuba would sell or lease land to the U.S. government so that military bases could be built on the island, including the establishment of a permanent U.S. naval base in Guantanamo Bay. A new president was sworn in in 1902, Don Tomas de Estrada Palma, a Cuban who had once favored the annexation of Cuba to the United States.

Many Cubans opposed the election of Estrada Palma, which they believed had not been carried out democratically. In the following years, the presidents that followed were not chosen by the people but "appointed" into office, men such as General J. Miguel Gomez and General Garcia Menocal. These "appointments" raised a great discontent among the Cuban people and provoked more insurrections. Labor strikes erupted all over the island, particularly in the sugar mills since sugar had become the basis of the island economy. Those strikes took place mostly between the years 1916 to 1921, forcing the United States to send reinforcements to Cuba.

By 1925 the United States owned and controlled almost the entire island, its banks, the transportation systems, the sugar cane fields and mills, the mines and the cattle, and the tobacco crops. In 1925, Gerardo Machado became the president of the Cuban Republic and remained in office until 1933 despite great public opposition. He formed his own personal army during his time in office and would order the death of anyone who would oppose him. He was responsible for the deaths of many student leaders and members of the underground movement. U.S. President Calvin Coolidge believed that Cuba was a sovereign state with freedom and democracy under the leadership of Machado.

In 1933, the Cuban opposition on the island organized a strike against Machado, which forced him to leave the island soon thereafter. Machado fled to the United States where he lived in exile until his death in 1939.

Machado was replaced by Carlos Manuel de Céspedes (son of the Cuban hero of the *"Ten Year War"*, and who was in favor of ending the "Platt Amendment". Because of his views, the United States government sought help from a Cuban army sergeant named Fulgencio Batista. Batista was asked to put Cuba back into its "proper place" and keep the "Platt Amendment" valid. Batista managed to overthrow Céspedes by organizing militarists and setting into action a revolt against him. Batista succeeded in his coup d'état on September fourth of 1933, thus forcing Carlos Manuel de Céspedes to resign.

In 1933, Batista was promoted to colonel for his accomplishment, while Grau San Martin became the next president, who was backed by Antonio Guiteras. Guiteras was a radicalized agitator but not a communist. Many new laws got to pass in Cuba thanks to Guiteras' influence on president Grau. Grau proceeded to abolish the "Platt Amendment", gave autonomy to all the universities, granted the workers the right to strike, and passed new laws regulating foreign profits. He even attempted to nationalize the United States owned electric company but failed. Batista was again called upon by the United States government for assistance in restoring order in the Cuban government. Antonio Guiteras was assassinated, which led to Grau's downfall since he depended so heavily on the advice of Guiteras for his policies.

From War to Rock 'n Roll

***

From 1935 until 1940, every man who held the office of the president of Cuba had indeed received fewer votes than the opposition candidates in rigged elections. They all promised many reforms for the people, promises that were never kept. Batista remained in office until 1944 when Grau took over the presidency once again.

In 1948, Carlos Prio Socarras was elected Cuba's next president. That same year, a group of distinguished Cubans who were against Prio Socarras decided to form the Orthodox Party. The main points of the Orthodox Party were; honor, political and economic independence and social justice.

The leader of the party, Eduardo Chivas, had about one-thousand followers. According to the polls, Chivas should have been elected into office in 1951, but the elections were rigged, and Batista was again nominated and placed into office. Because of the prevalent electoral corruption, Eduardo Chivas shot himself at the end of a radio speech as an appeal to the social consciousness of the people for freedom and justice. His last words were:

"I accuse the Prio government of having been the most corrupt government the Republic ever had" and then shot himself while on the air.

The impact of Chivas' action on the people was enormous. The founding of the Orthodox Party was what triggered my family's involvement in the cause of freedom for Cuba. My mother's father, Antonio Rodiles, was the first member of the family to join the party, followed by many other members of the family including both my mother and my father.

From War to Rock 'n Roll

Part One

My Introduction to
the Revolution

The Rodiles Family, mid 1950's

From War to Rock 'n Roll

1.

My Introduction to the Revolution

On March 10th, 1952 Batista staged a *coup d'état* and placed himself as the dictator of Cuba. That same year, he abolished the Cuban constitution of 1940, dissolved the congress, and outlawed the communist party while seeking aid from the United States. Most of the people on the island were dumbfounded by Batista's policies, who had been expected to bring about democracy to the island and not destroy it. Batista appeared not to care for the common people, but instead for those he considered in high standing in the Cuban society like the bankers, clergymen, property owners, American investors and industrialists.

In 1956, Fidel Castro Ruz, a law student who had tried unsuccessfully to get elected into office in previous years, was imprisoned for leading an armed attack to a military garrison in Santiago de Cuba. Fidel, whom was known to be a violent man at the university and who always packed a gun, decided to organize a guerrilla war to topple Batista's regime.

After being released from the maximum-security prison at Isle of Pines, Castro and his followers organized themselves in Mexico where they received military training by Alberto Bayo, an old communist combatant who had been defeated by Francisco Franco in the Spanish civil war. The leaders of the guerilla were Fidel Castro, his brother Raul and a foreigner "communist" known as Che Guevara. While in Mexico, Fidel, Raul and Che were also indoctrinated in Marxism and Soviet politics by Nikolai Leonov, a KGB officer stationed at the Soviet Embassy in Mexico City and with whom Raul had become good friends during a visit to the communist youth festival in Vienna in 1953.

In the end, Castro's revolution eventually won in 1959 at the cost of many lives and much suffering. While it initially brought a steady government that had the support of most of the people, everything changed on December 2, 1961. On that day, Castro proclaimed himself a communist, something that he had kept under wraps throughout guerilla war years. Castro had blatantly betrayed the fundamental principles of the revolution held by most people who fought alongside him or supported him.

On January 1st, 1959, dictator Fulgencio Batista fled to exile when his regime collapsed. As a result, Castro's instituted a Soviet-style totalitarian regime in Cuba that has remained in power unchanged until the present time.

From War to Rock 'n Roll

***

My story begins in 1952, in the southern limits of the city of Guantanamo, Cuba. At the time, my family lived at 1304 Maximo Gomez Street, a house owned by my grandfather who also owned the adjoining bakery, which was connected to our house by several entryways.

It was a close family compound. My grandfather lived in a smaller house in the back of the bakery and one of my uncles lived across the street from our house with his seven children, with whom I became were very close and spent much of my time playing on the streets.

My mother, Antonia Gonzales Rodiles, taught night classes at a primary school for illiterate adults. She went religiously to that school every night of the week to teach from nine o'clock until twelve o'clock. She often spoke to the family and to our most trusted friends of the political problems in our country and of the need for a radical change that would bring about equality to the people. She would also convey her thoughts to the students in her classes, regardless of the consequences that she would have faced had one of her students decide to report her political views to the authorities.

My mother also kept a heavy hand me, even though I always fought to be independent and was hard to keep in line. She would often punishd me for reasons that I did not understand at the time, but now I realize the importance for having a strict discipline early in life. Once I came to understand her reasons I realized that she was the greatest woman in the world.

When my father would leave the house to pick up my mother from work, usually between ten thirty and eleven thirty at night, one of my aunts would come to look after my younger sister, Grisel, and me. However, I often escaped from the house to meet with my cousins on the streets. Sometimes we would go to the railroad tracks near where we lived and ride the horses that the *campesinos* had left tied down for the night. We would just take them for a short ride and then either return them or set them free wherever we ended up at. Other times, also while in my aunt's care, I would spend time exploring the house, searching and poking through all the drawers and closets, just out of curiosity and looking for nothing in particular.

One night   while snooping around I noticed that the door to my father's closet was left ajar. That was one place that I haven't yet explored since my parents had always taken the pain to keep it locked. What I found there left me in awe.

I found several long guns inside that closet, which later I was told were high-power Springfield rifles. The moment I grabbed one to check it out, my father walked into the room and stood there paralyzed for a few seconds. He then took the gun from me and put it down on the floor. By then, my mother had also walked into the room and realized what was happening. Both seemed to be at a loss for words and so did I, expecting an angry reaction on their part. That was the first time in my life I had held a gun.

My parents told my sister Grisel to stay away from the room and then shut the door. Moments later, they started explaining all about those guns and why they were in there. They revealed to me, for the first time that both were members of a secret, subversive organization called the *26th of July*, which objective was the liberation of the people from the cruel dictatorship of Fulgencio Batista.

My parents told me that the 26th of July movement had got its name for the day when Castro and a group of followers attacked the Moncada army garrison in the city of Santiago de Cuba. The battle between the insurgents and Batista's soldiers left many people dead from both sides. Only thirty of the attackers survived this battle and Fidel was one of them. Fidel and others went into hiding but were either captured or forced to surrender to Batista's forces in the days that followed.

The Moncada "attackers" were tried in a court in Santiago de Cuba and sentenced to serve fifteen years in jail at the maximum-security prison of Isle of Pines. In response to the sentencing, the underground movement increased their sabotage activities in many cities, stormed a radio station to make a brief liberty broadcast, and even attacked the presidential palace in Habana.

Two years later, in 1955, Batista declared a general amnesty and freed Castro and all other jailed rebels. The amnesty was staged by Fidel's father in law, Rafael Diaz-Balart, who at the time was the majority leader at the house of representatives. The insurgents fled the country and reorganized themselves in Mexico, where they were joined by a self-proclaimed communist from Argentina called Ernesto Ché Guevara. The group received training in guerrilla tactics in Mexico and soon made plans to return to the island to carry out and organized fight against the government.

Their plan was to land in Cuba on the same day that other members of the movement were to carry out a huge protest in the city of Santiago de Cuba. Castro and his followers had also planned to capture the town of Manzanillo right after their landing. The group set off from Mexico in a battered 60-foot yacht called the "Granma" but due to a hurricane at sea they arrived in Cuba two days past their schedule and got driven off course by heavy winds.

Because of the storm, the expeditionary force landed by accident on a beach called *Las Coloradas*, a location that had been watched by Batista soldiers. As soon as the rebels hit the beach Batista's air force bombed and strafed the landing area. The expedition lost all their provisions and some of their men in the trip - only twelve of the eighty rebels who had travelled from Mexico survived the landing. Among those twelve survivors were Fidel Castro, Raul Castro, Ché Guevara and nine others.

The small group headed straight for the *Sierra Maestra*, a mountain range totally isolated from civilization. There, the men rested and set camp among the local people called "campesinos". It was in those mountains where Castro established his base of operations that lasted throughout the whole insurrectional war, and the place from where he directed the underground to carry out sabotages in the cities. Soon thereafter, many volunteers started heading for the mountains from all over the country to join Castro 's force.

My parents also told me that Batista's police and soldiers were carrying out assassinations under government's orders, targeting anyone suspected of being part of any of the subversive groups, particularly the 26th of July. As I listened, I knew that I had to keep my mouth shut about the guns to insure their safety. That night, I gained a better understanding of the political situation in Cuba and the injustice that Batista had brought upon the people.

The murders and injustices perpetrated by Batista regime fueled the people's resolve to fight back for their freedom, and for the lives of their friends and family. Cuba had again become a divided country. On one side was the government and its supporters against Fidel, and on the other Fidel and the majority of the people against the government.

While Batista's soldiers carried out their terror tactics, the rebels in the *Sierra Maestra* got organized, begun to grow their own food, built field hospitals and set up power and communication lines in the mountain towns and other areas under their control. The rebels spent much of their time studying about guerilla tactics to prepare themselves for the time when Batista forces would come to the mountains and try to root them out.

Day by day, I became more knowledgeable of the political situation in Cuba and more interested in taking part in the activities of the movement. The *26th of July* organization often held its secret meetings at our house, where I sat and listened to their discussions and got educated on the warfare tactics used by the members of the underground in all major cities and towns throughout the island.

My grandmother and Ché Guevara.
Guevara was an Argentinean assassin who went to Cuba
to murder Cubans and who the Castro dictatorship
later proclaimed as a hero.

***

My first direct involvement in the movement's activities happened in October of 1953 during a general strike staged by the workers in the province of Oriente. One day, my parents and other members of the organization were trying to smuggle guns to our house from another house where the guns would be stored until they could be transported safely. That house was only a few blocks away from ours, but there was a problem in getting them over. Batista's army had positioned one soldier on permanent guard less than fifty feet from our doorstep.

I offered to transport the guns but, almost everyone laughed until my mother intervened. She agreed with the idea that a young boy riding a bicycle through the streets would most likely not arise suspicions. I was given a piece of paper cut in half before I left the house to identify myself to the member who had the guns, then rode my bicycle to the designated house where I gave the man in charge my half of the paper. He showed me the other half of the paper and then produced the guns for me.

There were four guns in total, all twelve caliber shotguns. I made two trips, carrying two guns wrapped on jute sacks on each ride, and going right past the guard house without the soldier even taking notice of me. As my mother had predicted, I carried out my first assignment successfully. This started my first real involvement with the underground in the struggle against the government.

During the general strike of October there were two companies that decided not participate: the electric company and the railroad line that ran from Guantanamo to Caimanera. One night during the strike, two of my uncles, Samuel and Manuel Rodiles, along with four other members of the underground attacked the electric company with machine gun fire and put it out of commission. Two days after the attack, my other uncle Antonio Rodiles decided to do something to stop the train from running. He had suffered a case of malignant polio and had diffi-culty walking alone without any help, but he had the will to go through his plan.

Antonio was a student of law at the University of Santiago de Cuba at the time. He went to the railroad tracks about a mile away from the station and wrapped himself in a Cuban flag and laid himself down on the tracks, hoping that the conductor wouldn't murder him and desecrate a Cuban flag at the same time. Soon enough, the police arrived to take him off the tracks, causing a great commotion as they arrested him. Many students came to see what was going on and began to throw rocks at the police as Antonio was being taken away.

During the strike, one of Batista's generals, General Masferrer, was doing a radio broadcast to the people and talking about the overwhelming force of Batista's army, and of the superiority of the government over the insurgents. He was telling the people about the tactics that would be put into effect to stop the strike and to prevent any others from occurring. Batista felt it was necessary to remind the people constantly of his power through the voices of his most devote generals.

While General Masferrer was busy reading his speech, he didn't notice my uncle Samuel Rodiles entering the radio station carrying two of his homemade grenades. Samuel threw both grenades at the general's radio booth but neither of them exploded. He fled from the radio station while exchanging gunfire with the police. Samuel failed in his attempt to kill the general and destroy the radio station but, he did manage to escape from the police.

Samuel went straight to the mountains since he would never again be able to show his face in the city until Batista was out of office. He joined forces with the rebel army in an area called *Bayate,* which was under the command of commander Efijenio Almejeiras.

Commander Samuel Rodiles

A few days after the incident at the radio station, my mother was laid off from her job at the school by orders from the government and my grandmother's house was searched by a special unit of the army called the S.I.M., the Military Intelligence Services, which was notorious for carrying out political assassinations for the government. My uncle Manuel was arrested by the S.I.M. in a case of mistaken identity, for they believed he was Samuel Rodiles.

They took him away in a truck to the jail of Guantanamo and then the next day he was to be transferred to the jail in Santiago de Cuba.

When they loaded him into the truck the next day to be taken to Santiago de Cuba, we drove right behind them. In the car were my aunts, my grandmother and myself. We followed along behind the truck to be sure that he arrived safely in the city of Santiago de Cuba. It was well known that the people of S.I.M. would often stop along the way during the transfer of political prisoners and murder them in the road and leave them to be found with no explanation given, just coming up with some excuse like the prisoner being shot while attempting to escape. We made it obvious that we were following them so the S.I.M. officers could not murder my uncle without any witnesses.

Manuel did reach Santiago de Cuba safely and with the help of another uncle of mine, Salvador Rodiles, who was a teacher at the university, he was freed after one day.

The relief in my uncle's face as he rode with us back to Guantanamo made me realize that the situation could have turned out terrible had Salvador not been able to verify his identity to the police. He would have likely been killed for no reason at all, something they would have blamed to some "accident".

When we got back to Guantanamo, my parents were already making plans for Manuel and my father to leave the city and join the rebels in the mountains since they believed that the police were very close to finding out about their clandestine activities in the city. A shorth while later, my uncle Manuel Rodiles left for the mountains.

My father, on the other hand, decided to stay for a while longer so he could finish an important project he was working on. He had set up a grenade factory in our backyard where he used a furnace to melt down aluminum with the excuse of using it to mold holy objects. In reality, he poured the molten aluminum into our homemade grenade molds and then hid the finished grenades inside the house until they were ready to be distributed. The grenades that we made needed no chemicals to make them explode. Instead, they had a simple fuse inserted in the middle. When the fuse was ignited, the detonation was intense enough to force the grenade to blow up into many flying pieces of shrapnel.

We had hung a huge picture of our enemy, Fulgencio Batista, in our living room wall. My parents used it as a decoy to pretend our allegiance to the government in case the house was ever searched by soldiers, or by the police.

It was that picture what we believed saved us from being arrested in one occasion when the police came to our house searching for my maternal grandfather. As the police entered the house, the first thing that they saw was the picture of their leader hanging on the wall. This, along with my mother's hospitable demeanor surprised them very much and helped set aside their suspicions. I remember the sergeant in charge saying to the rest of the men there *"estan con el hombre"*, meaning, "they are with the man" - "the man" being Batista, of course.

Our family had duped the police into believing our fake allegiance to the government thanks to the picture in the living room, and our calm behavior. They left the house without even searching it and took our word that we had no idea of where my grandfather was. As soon as they left the house, we rushed to move the materials that we used to make the grenades, the guns that were hidden in the house and all the finished grenades out of there. We hid the grenade molds in a recess above the oven in the bakery of my paternal grandfather. My father gathered all the finished grenades and the guns and headed out to deliver them to the rebels in an area called *San Antonio del Sur* near Baracoa. That region was under the command of commander Felix Pena.

It took us about five hours to move all the incriminating evidence from the house, and for my father to leave. Soon enough, the police were back knocking at our door. Apparently, the soldiers who were there the first time and gave the report that the house was clear were severely reprimanded by their superiors and ordered to return and search the house. I counted eight of them barging through our front door. The only family members in the house at that time were my grand-aunt and me. Everyone else had gone elsewhere because they had a feeling that they would be coming back soon.

The police searched the entire house thoroughly this time around and they asked us repeatedly for the whereabouts of my grandfather, but we stuck to our denial the we had any knowledge of where he was. The soldiers found no evidence that we were involved with the underground or got any information from and had to leave empty handed once again.

My mother, my aunts and I remained in the city of Guantanamo for quite a while working with the underground. We had been assigned with the task of distributing the arms, ammunitions, medicines and bandages to the second front *Frank Pais*, a region in the mountains occupied by the rebel forces.

Frank Pais, who the second front was named after, had been an active leader of the underground and was part of the 26th of July attack to the Moncada barracks in Santiago de Cuba. Soon after the attack, Frank was taken from his house by the soldiers and murdered on the street. The public execution was intended to set an example to the rest of the members of the underground, the rebels, and people aiding the rebel's cause in any way. In response to Frank's murder, the people of Santiago staged a huge funeral for him, with almost everyone in the city attending. All the women were dressed in black and everyone carried either a poster or wore an armband with the words the *26th of July* printed on them.

The army was sent to disband the funeral procession, but it was all in vain. That day, the people on outnumbered the soldiers and the situation soon turned very explosive. Frank's funeral was carried out successfully showing that the people still had the will to fight back and protest for their freedom and would not be scared or forced into submission by terror tactics.

The second front *Frank Pais* consisted of four separate regiments of the rebel army. One was led by my uncle Samuel Rodiles and commander Efijenio Almejeiras, another by commander Felix Pena and commander Fajardo, in which my father had reached the rank of lieutenant. The leaders of the two other fronts were Manuel Piñeiro, alias Barbaroja, and Tomas Acebich.

We made many deliveries of the much-needed supplies from Guantanamo to the second front. The supplies were shipped from Santiago de Cuba through an underground network. As time went on, our trips to the mountains became more and more difficult because of the increased presence of soldiers patrolling the streets, which had forced us to take many back roads to elude them. We were spotted several times, but they let us through. I believed that what deterred the authorities from searching us was our appearance - a young boy travelling with two women who claimed to be teachers and had the papers to prove it.

One of my most traumatic experiences of the war happened while we were delivering supplies in a town called Mayari Arriba, the headquarters for the entire second front. We arrived in the town at about six o'clock in the morning and my mother had sent me straight to a farmer's house to get milk. That's when I heard people screaming "avion, avion", which meant that the town was about to be raided by planes. I looked up to the sky and saw a small Piper plane flying high up over the town. We knew that this plane wasn't used for attacks; it was equipped with a special detecting equipment that could locate radio transmitters on the ground as it flew over them. If the Piper scout plane discovered a town where a radio transmitter was located, they would radio in to the nearest air force base to scramble fighting planes to the scene and bomb the town.

As soon as the scout plane was spotted, some of the men ran to the house where the radio transmitter was installed. That radio was used regularly to send messages to other areas and to broadcast the rebel's propaganda to the cities and towns in the area. The men attempted to turn the radio off before it could be detected by the Piper but the sound of more planes heading in our direction later told us that it had been too late. The transmitter had been detected and the town would soon be under attack. Everyone started running for cover, in all directions and trying to gather their families to ensure they were all safe as the fighting planes arrived and opened fire on the town, dropping bombs and strafing with their machine guns.

Four planes took part in the attack on Mayari Arriba, two Sea Fury's, and two B-26's. The small Piper remained high above the scene observing the mayhem below.

My mother, my aunt and I had stayed together through all the confusion and then decided to run through a field and try to take cover on the other side of a fence. We made it to the fence, but we found a young boy who had been killed by the gunfire from the planes. He was just lying there, hanging from the fence. There wasn't anything that we could do for the boy and still had to reach safety ourselves and so we had no choice but to leave him there and go over the fence. Once on the other side, we started to run towards a ditch. As I was running, a chain with a cross that I was wearing around my neck and which belonged to my mother got caught on a tree branch and broke. As I turned to reach and grab it I saw bullets hitting the ground a few inches away. I quickly picked up the chain and ran towards the ditch where my mother and aunt had already taken refuge.

My mother was shaken. She thought I was going to get killed by one of the bullets that hit just a few inches from where I've been standing. She started crying and said that she wished that she had never gotten me involved in the war activities and exposed me to such danger. I tried to calm her down and told her that if we were to die there, then she would be crying over something that didn't even happen and wasn't worth it. I added that we should focus instead on getting out of that situation alive. I also told her that I felt the same way as the other rebels, that I believed that I was fighting for the right thing and that I was there on my own choice and no one had forced me to go.

My mother looked surprised to hear me say those words, but it did calm her down and then our attention turned my aunt Noemi, who was crying out loud in pain. She said that she could feel stinging bites all over her body. That's when we noticed that not only her body, but ours too were totally covered with ants. We had jumped straight into a huge colony of red ants whose bites are known to cause tremendous pain. The ants were biting us ferociously all over, but we didn't other choice but to stay put and battle them. It was a much more even match confrontation than leaving the ditch and being exposed to the planes that were shooting at us from above. The planes kept on firing on the town and on the surrounding areas for a few hours longer. They used a system where two of the planes would return to the air base to refuel while the other two stayed and continued to fire. Using this method, four the planes could attack one area for as long as they liked with no breaks.

We left the cover of the ditch once we noticed that the shooting had stopped and that the planes were not coming back. The town's people also started to emerge from their hideouts to check the damage that the planes had caused and to count the casualties.

The radio station, the main target of the attack, had been destroyed by a direct bomb hit. A radio operator inside had been killed in the explosion, while two other people had been wounded. Those were the only casualties known of so far, besides the young boy that we found dead in the field. The streets were covered with huge holes where the bombs had fallen and exploded, big enough to become swimming pool foundations.

When the rain started, they all got filled with water and turned indeed into swimming pools.

We moved into a shelter that had been set up to care for the wounded and for the town's people to gather inside and rest. The people of Mayari Arriba were lucky to make it through the attack with so few people dead or injured, but the damage that was done to their town was immense. Many homes had been destroyed, which meant that those families would have to reconstruct their lives from scratch. Most of the town's businesses were also ruined. A few days later, we decided it was time to head back to Guantanamo, leaving the people of Mayari Arriba in a distraught state as they tried to put their town and their lives back together.

On our way back to Guantanamo we stopped in a village called *Bayate*, where the sixth column of the second front had set up their headquarters. First in command was commander Efijenio Almejeiras and the second in command was my uncle Samuel Rodiles. We spent only one day there and again we were on the road back to Guantanamo.

Upon our return to Guantanamo, my mother and I were dropped off at our house, while my aunt Noemi was to get off the jeep a few blocks from my grandmother's house where she lived. We were certain that her house had been under surveillance since the day of my uncle's arrest. She was also wary of a captain in Batista's police who lived directly across the street from her. My aunt Noemi feared having to face the police captain and try to explain to him why she was returning home in a jeep covered with mud that had obviously been on a long trip in the country.

Back in the safety of our home, I started to reflect on everything that I had learned since I found those guns in my father's closet and the lessons that he gave me on Cuban politics. By then, I thought that it was the duty of every man to fight for what he believed was right. In my young mind, I felt totally committed to the rebel's cause and was willing to die for it, as it nearly happened during several of our delivery trips to the mountains.

But I also realized that what I really needed was music. Listening to music had become the most calming part of my life and helped clear my mind from the images of death that were always outstanding in my memory. I had become too familiar with death, but I still found it hard to accept. Music, though, seemed to be there the least of my time and I wondered if there ever would be a time when music would occupy all my time, with death now being such an imminent threat to us. I didn't know then that for me to make music my whole life I would have to leave Cuba someday. I wouldn't find out about this until after Castro's regime came into power, when my interest in rock n 'roll grew day after day while listening to the Miami radio stations and realized that this great phenomenon known as Rock 'n Roll was happening in the world, but mostly in the United States.

Within a few days after our return to the city we got a phone call from two of my uncles, Antonio and Juan Gonzales Rodiles who were at the university in Santiago de Cuba. Juan was studying medicine and Antonio wanted to become a lawyer. They wanted to know about the movement's progress in Guantanamo and how the family was making out. They had decided to leave their studies temporarily and return to Guantanamo to join us in the resistance.

Miguel Garcia, an uncle on my father's side, agreed to have both my other uncles stay with him. A few days after the arrangements were set, Antonio and Juan arrived in the city safely and immediately began plotting new tactics to carry out the urban guerilla fight. They believed that those tactics could effectively advance the revolution at a faster pace.

Their idea was to engage in the disruption of the local economy and hopefully the regime of Batista along with it. Those tactics were indeed violent but regarded as a necessary evil. Members of the underground started placing bombs in the city, mostly in businesses establishments and set them to go off at a certain time. The people of Guantanamo were told to stay off the streets after a certain hour, the time when the bombs were set to explode, thus enacting a curfew to keep the citizens away from the business establishments. My family was placed in charge of directing these activities in the city of Guantanamo.

2.

Deliveries to the Rebels in the Mountains

Some of the supplies destined for the second front *Frank Pais* were to be distributed in the areas of Baracoa and Yateras, both under the command of commander Felix Pena. In one occasion, my mother, my aunt and myself loaded the jeep with supplies and took off for Baracoa along with another rebel, *Tanganyika*, who got his nickname after a character in a popular radio soap opera. Tanganyika had been assigned to be our driver for this trip. We left at three o'clock in the morning and traveled on every back road available to avoid the soldier patrols and the risk of being searched. As we got to a town called Boquerón Tanganyika decided to drive through the cemetery in the outskirts of town for he feared that someone might spot us and report us to the authorities. From Boquerón, we headed towards Jateritas beach, in the direction of Baracoa and our ultimate destination that day.

By way of my mother and aunt's femininity, and the apparent innocence of a child, we were able to fool several army patrols and succeed in smuggling supplies to the rebels. They would tie show bags around their waists like aprons and hide them under their flared style dresses that were the fashion in those days. The twelve caliber shotgun shells that we carried fitted perfectly in the shoe bags, which allowed us to carry a large number on every trip. The medical supplies were also placed inside the bags and hid under the dresses.

The shotgun shells that we transported to the rebels had been refilled with heavier, larger pieces of lead rather than the small birdshot pellets they came with. We had made a special mold to form the large pellets by pouring molten lead into it. The larger ammunition we produced caused more damage and covered a much larger distance when fired. These were particularly effective in an ambush type combat, which the rebels had been employing in the mountains. The *hunters* could take on large numbers of enemy soldiers with shotguns by surprising them in ambush-style attacks.

About three miles before arriving to Jateritas beach Tanganyika had to stop to fill-up the Jeep's radiator which had run out of water. We got off the road and drove underneath a bridge where we saw a running stream from which we could collect the water. As we drove out from under the bridge we noticed a group of soldiers heading in our direction. The soldiers immediately signaled us to stop.

The men started asking us where we were going to and why? My mother told the officer in charge that we were on our way to open a small school in Baracoa where she and my aunt were to be the teachers. Both she and my aunt showed them their papers to prove they were certified teachers. Although the soldiers seemed to have believed in their story, they still went on and searched the jeep.

When Tanganyika saw that the soldiers were ready to intercept us, he slipped a thirty eighth caliber pistol into the back of my pants. I stood directly in front of him during the whole episode so that if he had the need he could quickly go for the gun. My aunt had begun to act out stomach pains so that her slow movements wouldn't catch the attention of the soldiers and cause any suspicions. She was carrying the 12 caliber shotgun shells and had to move slowly to keep them from making a rattling noise inside the bags. My mother was carrying mostly medicines and bandages and didn't have to worry about how she moved about. They didn't search our bodies and we were safe once again after a very close call indeed.

Arriving in the jeep to the eighteenth coumn.

Commander Fajardo, Ñiqita Rodiles and Felix Pena.

Once again, we were driving on the back roads on our way to Jateritas for our rendezvous with our contact at a beach house, which had been occupied by the rebels. The area of Jateritas was indeed the borderline point between the rebel forces and Batista's forces.

Our contact at the beach house advised us on which roads were safe to travel on our way to Baracoa and gave the password that we would have to use if were to be intercepted by the rebels. We spend one night at the beach house and left early the morning for our next destination, San Antonio del Sur. We had been driving for about three hours when we heard planes coming in our direction. We got off the road to camouflage the Jeep with tree branches and then took cover in the bush. The planes flew at a very low altitude above us but didn't spot us or the jeep and then kept on flying in the direction of Baracoa.

We sighted in relief after our second close call with death in one day. We were very nervous and decided to go around the city of San Antonio del Sur. Our contact at the beach house told us that San Antonio was held by Batista's forces and that there were soldiers crawling all over the place. Our next contact point was to be about five miles outside of the city of San Antonio del Sur, still in the direction of Baracoa.

Our contact at Jateritas beach had also warned us of an ambush that the rebel forces had planned on one of Batista's army columns that were headed to Baracoa. The ambush was to take place at a mile-long, narrow gorge flanked by steep mountains known as *el Abra de Mariana*.

As we got near this place we heard a voice yelling, *"Alto, quien viene?"* ("Stop, who's coming?") We answered the call with the password that our beach contact had told us to use, *"Libertad o muerte* ("Liberty or Death"). As soon as he heard our reply he knew that we were friendlies and allowed us to pass through. At the end of the road we ran into my father, who was there to take part on the ambush. We unloaded the supplies and were told by my father to take cover at the top of the mountain on the side of the road. There, we saw a group of rebel soldiers next to several barrels of gasoline, which they planned to ignite and dump down on top of the army regiment as they passed through the canyon.

A second group of rebels were to block the entrance after the regiment was inside the gorge, and the last group would position itself at the exit. Once the soldiers were inside the gorge, they would be trapped with no way out. All the rebels had to do now was to wait for the armored column to arrive.

My Father Guillermo Garcia.

El Abra de Mariana gorge.

Six hours later, the alert was given, and everyone got ready for the ambush. We could hear the sound of tanks in the distance heading towards the gorge. As soon as the last vehicle had entered the gorge, the rebels opened fire. At the same time, the gasoline containers were ignited and allowed to roll down the steep hills. Taken by surprise, the soldiers began running with no place to take cover from the gunfire and the burning gasoline that was raining on them. They couldn't escape at either end of the canyon because the rebels had blocked both exit points. There were about three hundred soldiers in the military convoy, two tanks and a few Jeeps equipped with thirty caliber machine guns mounted on top.

The soldiers in Batista's regiment had M-1's and Springfield rifles, but our shotguns with specially recharged shells were much more effective in that type of ambush. The battle lasted for only an hour and it turned out to be a slaughter for all the Batista regiment at the gorge. There were no survivors, only a sickening smell of burning human flesh that permeated the air all around the area as the bodies burned away with the gasoline. I felt sick to my stomach and, to this day I can still smell the burnt human flesh when I think of that gruesome episode. It was April 16, 1958.

Shortly after the battle ended, Batista's air force planes appeared and opened fire on us. We ran to take cover in caves on the side of the mountain for a few days while the attack lasted. They were using the same method as in Mayari Arriba, in which one set of aircraft bombed away while another set went back to refuel and leaving us no chance to move away. Luckily, there was a running stream of water in the caves that we could use to drink, but when we ran out of food we had no other choice but to kill a few of our Mules for meat.

When the air attack ceased we could see the buzzards that had already begun to feast on the dead bodies that were left scattered all over the ground and the terrible odor of burnt human flesh that still hung in the air as the bodies smoldered away. We collected all the guns and ammunition that hadn't been destroyed by fire, and even took the boots off some of the corpses because some of the rebels didn't have any proper foot wear for the rocky terrain that could cut into their feet like sharp teeth. We managed to salvage one of the Jeeps that had a thirty-caliber machine gun mounted on it. All the other vehicles had been destroyed beyond repair by the fire.

We continued on our way after the battle accompanied by many of the rebels, while about thirty of them stayed behind with a radio unit so that they could relay messages ahead if they spotted any soldiers coming toward Baracoa. On our way, we were spotted by a small Piper plane of the Batista Air Force and had to split up to take cover. From our hiding place, one of the rebels took a shot at the plane and made a direct hit, sending the plane plummeting towards the ground. We set off again after another victory for the rebels.

Soon thereafter we reached the town of *Puriales de Caujerí* were a rebel hospital had been established. In command of the small hospital was commander Dr. Cervantes, who I met personally for the first time during this visit. In the hospital was a rebel who had been very badly, not in battle, but burned during an explosion in one of the rebel's bomb factories. He had been the only survivor of the blast. His name was Machito and I knew him personally from Guantanamo. As I entered the hospital the smell of burnt human flesh filled my senses and brought back vivid scenes of the ambush I had just witnessed.

My mother delivering a thirty-caliber machine gun to the rebels.

Dr. Gilberto Cervantes.

The rebel hospital in Puriales, Cuba ran by
Dr. Gilberto Cervantes

A few hours after we had arrived in Puriales we were served a meal at a kitchen across from the hospital. Despite my great hunger I couldn't eat a bite of food, for the cooked meat that they served me reminded me of the burnt bodies at el *Abra de Mariana.*

On the morning of the day that we were to depart from Puriales, I was approached by commander Felix Pena who presented me with a forty-four-caliber revolver in tribute to my being the youngest rebel soldier in the rebel army and for my dedication to their cause. I was close to nine years old at this time and felt that I was already a man carrying a man's responsibilities. I left that town with a very good feeling about myself. I felt honored and proud. Again, we started off for we still had to meet with Raul Castro and his secretary Vilma Espin, who had been performing a complete inspection of the second front and would soon arrive to a place near the town of Baracoa.

When we finally got to Baracoa we were informed that we were to meet Raul Castro at a small coffee plantation known as Bejuquera. The only way to get to Bejuquera was using mules to climb up the steep cliffs of that area. When we arrived in Bejuquera, Raul Castro gave my mother lists of needed supplies for all the areas of the second front that he had collected. He also gave her some secret documents, which were to be delivered to Fidel Castro at the first front in La Sierra Maestra, just outside the city of Santiago de Cuba. We spent three days with Raul Castro and Vilma Espin in Bejuquera and then came time for us to return to the city of Guantanamo. Once back home my mother gave the papers for Fidel to a rebel messenger to take them to the first front, then she began to gather all the supplies on the list so that they could be delivered to the second front as soon as possible.

Raul Castro and myself in the mountains of Oriente, Cuba.

3.

In the Mountains with the Rebels

Three months had passed from the time I had discovered the guns in my father's closet. I had been on a virtual three-month-long "vacation" and was now expected to return to school. At the time, I was attending an American school called Sara Asher whose director was an American missionary lady named Miss Clancy. I was due to go back to school only days after we returned to Guantanamo from our trip to Baracoa. All my classes from the first grade to the third grade were in English rather than in Spanish. Because Cuba's close trade ties with the United States, the school board believed that it was important for the students to learn how to speak English properly.

After I returned to school to resume my studies, the memories of the war left no room in my mind for school work. I became rebellious and one day wrote on the blackboard "long live the 26th of July". One of the teachers caught me in the act and threatened to turn me into the authorities. Although she didn't follow through with her threat, she scared me very much.

When I told my mother of the incident she became very concerned, but still she thought that school was still the safest place for me since most of the students at Sara Asher were from upper class families. However, it was hard for me to concentrate on my studies since I could not stop thinking of all that had happened during my trip to Baracoa.

Eventually, my mother decided that I should leave school for the duration of the war. From that day on, I went to live with my father's brother Miguel, where my two uncles who had come from Santiago de Cuba were also staying.

During their stay in Guantanamo, my uncles were put in charge of directing all the subversive activities that took place in the city. They would decide where the bombs were to be placed, and always made every effort to keep civilians safe from the blasts. A few times I helped them deliver the explosives to the individuals in charge of planting them at night. They would give me a bag with the bomb inside and I would deliver them to the assigned place for pick up. I often delivered messages for them too. Soon, we learned that Miguel's house was being watched by the police, so we had to be very careful on how we carried anything out of his house.

One night, a member of the underground named Omar Ranedo left Miguel's house and went to a coffee shop in a nearby park called "Jose Marti Park of Guantanamo" where he was arrested by the police and charged with possession of a revolver. While in police custody, Omar was brutally murdered. He was found in the cemetery outside the city, his body mutilated beyond recognition. The police had obviously tortured him to get information before killing him. They had ripped each of his finger nails out, he had been castrated with barbed wire wrapped around his balls, nails had been driven deep into his head, and was ultimately strangled with a strand of barbed wire.

Omar's body was identified by the special innersoles that his mother always put in his shoes. Omar had been a very important member of the movement and knew many names of members of the movement and all the key plans. None of our plans were disrupted after his arrest, which told us he had died a brave death to the end while enduring torture at the hands of the police. We carried out our activities out of my uncle's Miguel's house for a short time afterwards, but then decided that it was better for us to leave the city and join the fight in the mountains. After my uncles left I had to wait until someone could accompany me to the *Columna 18* of the second front were my father was deployed. My uncle Juan Rodiles, who had been studying medicine at University of Santiago de Cuba, went to the small town of Bayate to set up a field hospital for the rebels. My other uncle, Antonio Rodiles, who had been studying to be lawyer, went to Calabasar de Sagua to act as a judge in a military court that had been established there by the rebels. Both uncles were to take part in the fighting. A week after they had both left Miguel's house I also got my chance to leave.

Dr. Juan Rodiles and his brother Samuel Rodiles

A fresh shipment of supplies arrived in Guantanamo for delivery to the second front in Baracoa, where my father was deployed. This time, my mother brought me along on the trip together and she drove the Jeep herself. We were delivering mostly green camouflage uniforms, boots and some ammunition. Our trip went smoothly, and we didn't run into an army or a police patrol, but the driving was very difficult for my mother to handle. The roads were muddy, and there were steep cliffs on both sides. She had a very hard time keeping the vehicle from sliding in the mud and going over the edge. We had to make the trip during the night which didn't make it any easier for her. My mother, however, manage to get us to our destination safely.

As my mother and I were ready to go back to Guantanamo, I begged her to stay with us and not to return to the city because the police suspected her to be a member of the underground and was watching her. We all agreed that it wasn't safe for her to continue making the deliveries. It would be just a matter of time before she would be caught and arrested by the police.

My mother insisted to us that her work was too important for her to stop now and that there wasn't anyone else to do her job. She just refused to stop making the trips to the mountains and so we said goodbye and she left for Guantanamo to prepare for her next delivery. She also told us that she would dye her hair a different color every few weeks to disguise herself.

I stayed in Bejuquera with my father for about a week until he was transferred to *El Uvero* beach where a rebel training school had been set up and where he was to become one of the instructors. This beach had been held by Batista's men only a few months earlier until commander Felix Pena and his forces successfully took control of it.

Once we were at the school I would often sit in on the training classes to learn about the art of combat and ambush fighting. The instructors were all experienced rebel soldiers who had taken part in many battles. El Uvero was a good location, far away from the fighting and right on the water, allowing us to spend much of our free time at the beach. They also taught politics at the school so that the students understood that the purpose of the revolution was to bring about a democracy in Cuba and to restore the constitution of 1940, which Batista had arbitrarily abolished.

One day, everyone was asked to gather inside one of the classrooms and we were given of our orders to attack the town of Imias which had recently been fallen into Batista's army control. The battle had been planned for the following day and everyone was assigned their individual responsibilities for that battle. There were about sixty of us, but we were to receive re-enforcements before the start of the attack. Commander Felix Pena and his forces were to meet us on our way to our intended target, the town of Imias.

The next day we left at about six o'clock in the morning. We traveled in three trucks and two jeeps and it took us close to eleven hours of driving before we reached the point where we were to meet our re-enforcements. I rode in one of the jeeps with my father and four other men. One of them was a good friend of mine, a sergeant nicknamed *Sierra Alta*, who was later on killed during the battle. We eventually met with Pena's troops, where I was greeted by many friends whom I've got to know while making the deliveries with my mother and my aunts.

I also saw my good friend Juan Manual Tames and was happy to see that he had made it to the rank of lieutenant. Our orders stated that the battle was to begin at two o'clock on the following day. We all headed towards Imias and then set up a radio base about four miles outside the town's city limits. There, Felix Pena and our commander got together to discuss the strategies that we would be using for the attack.

At two o'clock in the morning of the next day, the rebels got ready to move in on the town, but I was ordered to stay behind at the radio base. I was disappointed for I wanted to go with the rest of them, but by staying behind at least I would know what was going on during the fighting through radio contact.

The rebels took their positions outside the city close to the fortress where Batista's soldiers had gathered for protection. Once all the rebels had moved to their positions, the order of attack was given, and everyone opened fire on the fort. Seconds after the shooting had started, the electrical power went off in the whole town. The people of Imias could be seen running all over the town trying to gather together their families to get to a safe location.

Our commanders knew that the battle had to be over with as soon as possible so that Batista's soldiers couldn't radio in for re-enforcements. The rebel troops under commander Efijenio Almejeiras and under my uncle, commander Samuel Rodiles were at the time fighting Batista's navy at the town of Caimanera. We sent them a message over the radio that we needed help. They responded that they had won their battle at Caimanera and were on their way to us.

Our re-enforcements arrived at Imias at about five o'clock on the following morning. Our forces had been fighting for nearly twenty hours and were both exhausted and running out of ammunition. The fort that the Batista army had for shelter appeared to be impossible to penetrate with our bullets. The reinforcements had brought along the only mortar they had, fired it and made a direct hit on the fort's wall, knocking it down and forcing the enemy into our range of gunfire. Batista's soldiers came out of the fort carrying a white flag and dropping their weapons as they emerged from their shelter.

Our forces took a great deal of supplies that Batista's army had stored inside the fort. There was also a large cache of weapons and ammunitions. Many of Batista's soldiers had joined the army just for the monthly pay they received, but secretly believed in the rebel's cause. Often, they were issued a gun by the army and then turn around and join the rebel forces. Because of the shortage of weapons, the rebel army required that every person who wanted to join brought his own weapon.

From War to Rock 'n Roll

While we suffered only a few casualties, I heard the bad news that my friend *Sierra Alta* had been killed, which upset me greatly. Since we did not have a facility to keep the prisoners taken at Imias, we set them free. Our mission had been accomplished; we had taken control of Imias and got all the supplies that the army had in storage.

Next to the broken wall on the fort we found the body of a soldier who called himself *Choncholy* who had been harassing the rebels verbally from inside the fort. He had been trying to break the moral of the rebels by screaming things like "I am Choncholy and I fucked all your mothers and wives so come and get me, mother fuckers" and then he would fire a few rounds of ammo from a window. His yelling didn't affect the rebel's moral at all they just figured that he was crazy we didn't take much notice until he was found dead. Even the sight of his dead body, his head torn open and a dog eating part of his brain brought remorse to some of the rebels, because most felt that regardless the political beliefs an adversary might have they still hated to kill him. Nobody was proud of killing, but it was war and there was no other choice left.

The three rebel groups loaded up the supplies that we had split and parted from Imias. I was glad for the chance to see my uncle Samuel who had just been honored with the rank of *commander* because of his bravery in the battle at Caimanera with commander Efijenio Almejeiras and his troops. Almejeiras started towards the area of Bayate with his men. Commander Felix Pena headed for the town of Puriales de Caujerí, which was his headquarters and our group returned to El Uvero Beach.

The rebel attacks on the government forces was taking place with more frequency all over the province of Oriente, putting a big dent on Batista's strength. Near Santiago de Cuba, Commander Juan Almeida had been ambushing troop convoys and causing much damage to the army. In the province of Santa Clara, toward the center of the Island, the rebels were successfully taking control of the area. In between the regions of Santiago de Cuba and Santa Clara, commander Hubert Matos and commander Juan Almeida were making great progress. In all the cities, members of the underground were carrying out their subversive activities and causing tremendous damage by sabotaging the electric company plants, the sugar cane mills, and burning down the plantations.

Meanwhile, the underground was also making assassination attempts of government officials. The regime was realizing more and more that was losing control over the island. Rebel forces were fighting now with greater will as they saw their victory coming closer to reality.

Batista, as a last resort, went on murdering and torturing of citizens who were suspected of helping the rebels or the underground movement in any way. Meanwhile, the communications between Batista's army regiment all over the country, particularly in the oriental province, had been almost totally cut off completely by the rebel forces. Batista's army supplies, including their weapons, ammunition, and documents were being systematically intercepted by the rebels. In a desperate effort to regain control, the army armed a specially designed bullet proof train covered with heavy metallic plates. They loaded the train with soldiers, heavy artillery and supplies and tried to get it from Havana to Oriente. Through our underground sources, the rebels learned of his plan and were able to set up an ambush for the train. The rebels knew that if they could stop and destroy this train, it could mean the end of Batista's dictatorship and the end of the war.

The rebel regiments that were assigned to this ambush mission were under the command of the most experienced fighting commanders in the entire rebel army - the men who had lead the most important battles of the war. They were Juan Almeida, Guevara, Hubert Matos, Efijenio Almejeiras, and Samuel Rodiles. Meetings were held to discuss strategies how the attack was to be carried out. All the rebel troops under their command were deployed to the province of Santa Clara, the place where the train was to be ambushed. The heaviest weapons the rebels had at the time were some mortars and some small cannons.

After a long battle, the rebel regiments succeeded in stopping and destroying the train. A very good friend of mine and great warrior, Asdrabal Lopez Sain, lost his life during this battle which made me very sad for a long time. Batista's last attempt to get his supplies through to the oriental side of the island had failed. As a result, the rebel army now had a huge cache of weapons and ammunition recovered from the train. Most of the soldiers that were captured in this battle were set free except some officers charged with war crimes.

A month later, on January 1, 1959 while I was still at the Uvero Beach tactical combat school, we received the news that Batista and a few of his associates had boarded a plane and fled the island. The news traveled quickly all over Cuba and the people were surprised of hearing that our victory had happened so soon. All over celebrations of the victory were being held and the rebel forces preparing to return to their homes and rejoin their families. Many soldiers and officers of Batista's army kept the war going, but it didn't take long for the rebels to defeat these forces and court martial them.

The Rodiles Family

Asdrubal Lopez Sain.

Me in the mountains of Oriente.

Capture of the fort of Guantanamo after Batista had fled. Here my aunt No-emi, my mother Ñiqita, my father Guillermo Garcia and myself with a group of the rebels.

With my family and friends

From War to Rock 'n Roll

I was present at one of the trials for the war criminals that were held in Guantanamo. Many of the officers that were being tried on that day were guilty of murdering and torturing young students from the city of Guantanamo. Two of the officers being tried on this day were Aguero and Granado; those men had murdered and tortured many people. They were sentenced to death. When they were taken to be executed, one of them tried to take a gun from one of the rebel guards who was escorting them, which triggered the rebels to open fire on them right there inside the truck. The mothers of the victims who had been shot by those officers began to attack their dead bodies in anger beating on them with great hatred. The trials that were being held all over the island marked the end of Batista's regime and all his puppet, money hungry soldiers. The rebels had now made their way to form a new military government with Castro as their leader and secure what everyone then believed would be a "free and democratic Cuba".

Samuel Rodiles.

My mother with Raul Castro.

Left to right: Manuel Rodiles, Antonio Rodiles, Juan Rodiles, Samuel Rodiles, and Rosa Rodiles Planas.

Samuel, Ñiquita, Piñeiro, and Guillermo Garcia.

Me with my uncle Samuel Rodiles and his bodyguards.

From left to right:
Samuel Rodiles, Ñiquita Rodiles (my mother), Manuel "Barbaroja"
Piñeiro, and my father, Guillermo Garcia.

Samuel Rodiles y Julio Casas Regueira.

Commander Camilo Cienfuegos.

Commander Samuel Rodiles.

*Gathering of the rebels receiving supplies from my mother, Ñiquita Rodiles,
and aunt, Noemi Rodiles.*

Ammunition factory in the mountains.

En Máximo Gómez 1,304 (Guantánamo) existía un arsenal para los revolucionarios, el lugar donde se depositaban las armas.

A weapon cache in Guantanamo.

Noemi Rodiles and Raul Castro

The vast majority of Cuba's population was intoxicated with Fidel Castro's victory until he declared himself a Communist.

From War to Rock 'n Roll

Part Two

Construction of
Cuba's Socialistic Republic

From War to Rock 'n Roll

1.

Creation of Cuba's New Government

In 1959, my family was transferred to the island's capital, La Habana. I was eleven years old then and for the following year I was sent to attend a private military academy affiliated with the government - the *Military Academy of the Caribbean.* The academy offered both academic and sports subjects and it wasn't long before I became the fencing champion at that school.

The academy life helped me greatly in coping with my memories of the war. While it was a military school with respect to the strict discipline that was imposed to the cadets, there were no combat training courses. My parent's main goal in enrolling me in this school had been to take my mind away from the war and to help me make up for the lost academic years back in Guantanamo. At times, though, I couldn't help but to think of the loss of my friends and all the death that I had witnessed. My father was named Captain Inspector of the police for the entire country and my uncle Samuel was the second chief of police. The police building where my father worked at was very close to my school therefore he was able to visit me almost every day.

In the very first government after the takeover, the council of Ministers named Manuel Urrutia Lleó as President of the island and José Miro Cardona was named as Prime Minister. At this time, most businesses of Cuba we still privately owned. The Urrutia–Cardona government lasted only six weeks until Miro Cardona was forced to resign, and Fidel Castro took the office of Prime Minister.

Fidel Castro began to make reforms as soon as he took over office. His first move was the called the "Agrarian Reform." Under this new law, the government was given *carte blanche* to confiscate all the private land, big and small, and eliminate all large land holdings. While the land was supposed to be re-distributed to those who would work it, the government remained in full control of the land and all the produce harvested therein. The *National Institute of Agrarian Reform*, the INRA, came to existence which turned the island economy into a total disaster.

The then United States president, Dwight Eisenhower, was a Republican, therefore the Democratic Party in the United States became very anti-communist because of Castro's radical actions. John F. Kennedy manipulated the Cuban issue as one of his main campaign points while running for the presidency in 1960. He blamed the Republican Party for allowing Castro to come into power on the island.

A few months after Castro issued the "agrarian reform" law, an "urban reform" law was also put into effect. Under this new law, all the real estate on the island was confiscated from private hands by the government and the tenants would only pay half of the rent that they had been paying in the past. Transportation costs were also lowered, along with medical costs and all the private beaches and Country Clubs were outlawed. At that time, the United States still had a lot of investments inside Cuba.

The Cuban people were happy with Fidel's new laws and reforms but didn't want a communist government to make those reforms for them. Because of the growing discontent over Castro's plan to institute a soviet-style communist regime, many rebel commanders felt betrayed by Fidel and moved to the Escambray mountains to fight against the new regime. To many of those rebel officers, communism was not what Castro had promised while leading the revolution in the Sierra Maestra.

I was personally very confused about all those changes since I had been told that the new government was going to be a true democracy. The insurgent war in the Escambray mountains against Castro was eventually suffocated and Castro moved with an iron fist to consolidate his totalitarian control over Cuba.

Before the uprising, Castro's puppet president Manuel Urrutia announced that all the communists would be purged from the government. Soon thereafter Fidel resigned as prime minister in a well-staged sham. Days after Fidel left office, the people demanded Urrutia's resignation as president and had Fidel return as prime minister. The council of ministers the nominated Osvaldo Dorticos Torrado to take Urritia's place as president. Dorticos was not a communist but he was also another puppet of Castro. When Dorticos decided to commit suicide, Fidel started running the whole show by himself.

In 1960, the Soviet Union began to move in. It was the culmination of a long-term, obscure conspiracy that had started many years earlier at the USSR embassy in Mexico City. The soviets rushed to offer to send oil to Cuba in exchange for a quota of sugar at a set market price. They were also promised the advent of a communist regime on the island allied with the USSR.

Almost immediately, Cuba Castro nationalized all the American-owned refineries and businesses on the island, along with all the businesses owned by Cuban nationals. The implementation of the feared Soviet-style totalitarian state had just started.

From War to Rock 'n Roll

***

In April of 1961, while still at the Military Academy of the Caribbean, I joined the campaign for ratification of illiteracy on the island. I became part of about one hundred and twenty students whom had been trained Varadero Beach in modern methodology to teach adults how to read and write. I was twelve years old when the campaign began and left the Academy for eight months to take part in this program.

On April 15th, 1961, several B-26 planes painted with Cuban Air Force insignias on them and piloted by Cuban exiles left from bases in Central America and flew over La Habana and other Cuban cities with the mission to bomb Castro's airfields. Their purpose was to wipe out all the combat planes that the Cuban air force had in those bases throughout the island.

The explosions at the airport of Ciudad Libertad in Havana were heard by most people in the city. When my father and I heard the blasts, we grabbed our guns and drove to the airport thinking that an invasion had begun. When we arrived at Libertad, we watched the B-26 planes bombing and strafing the runways and the airport buildings. There were planes on fire all over the airfield, many of which had been destroyed. Others were left in poor condition and unable to fly. After the air raid was over, we stayed over to help with the wounded. Then I returned to the Academy with my father and went back to the central police building.

2.

- Bay of Pigs invasion and the Cuban Missile Crisis –

On April 17, 1969, a state of alert was sounded throughout the island. A battalion of Cubans living in exile had started an invasion of the island in the swamps of Zapata, or *Cienaga de Zapata,* an area also known as *Playa Giron.* Some of the invaders arrived on cargo ships converted into military transports, while others were dropped by parachute from C-47 airplanes. The goal of the invasion was to create a beachhead in Cuba and form a provisional government that would request, and then be given recognition and support by the United States. Meanwhile, the military forces of the island were accustomed to a guerrilla style warfare and were not trained to defend against a full-scale invasion.

At ten o'clock in the morning on the first day of the invasion, my father came to the academy to say goodbye before he went to fight in Playa Girón. I told him that I wanted to go with him and take part in the fight, but he had just come to say goodbye and told me that I was to stay at the academy, and to fight for it if it was necessary. My father was in a police force battalion led by commanders Efijenio Almejeiras and Samuel Rodiles. The men who made up this battalion were seasoned fighters from the days of the insurgent war and had orders from Castro to stop this invasion. They would be conducting a deferent type of fighting this time around, though.

A whole battalion of Cuba's militia traveling by bus to Playa Giron was decimated as they came near the invader's landing area. They were specialized teams that had been trained in the use of anti-aircraft artillery and were responsible for stopping the enemy planes. They had four barrels, 14,5 mm Chinese anti-aircraft machine guns, and thirty-seven-millimeter anti-aircraft cannons from Czechoslovakia.

The invaders had begun their advance on the highway to Jaguey Grande when the police battalion arrived and drove them back. Many officers from this battalion were killed and others wounded. Meanwhile, the few planes left from the Cuban air force had been attacking and sinking the transport ships, and also strafing the invaders that were advancing slowly on the swamps. Less than seventy-two hours after the start of the invasion, the Cuban exiles were forced to surrender.

Twelve hours after the battle begun, my mother and my two ants left for Playa Giron to provide aid to the wounded. One of my uncles had been shot, but Samuel and my father came out of the fight unscratched.

After the bay of Pigs invasion, Cuban started receiving the first shipments of ground artillery and MIG jet fighters from the Soviet Union and China. A secret agreement was signed between Cuba and Russia stating that the Soviet Union would help defend the Cuban Marxist revolution against any future foreign invasions.

Once the Cuban-Soviet alliance became publicly known, Cuba was expelled from the OAS, the Organization of American States. The CIA kept many of the Bay of Pigs veterans on their payroll for more than a decade afterward. The U.S. government was looking for different ways to topple Castro government. It wasn't until seven years after the Bay of Pig invasion that the CIA finally closed its two largest training bases in Florida, where the Cuban refugees had received training to act against Cuba. One of those bases was located at an old naval air station at Opa-locka, which had served as an all-purpose base for CIA sponsored raids against Cuba.

Raul Castro in the Soviet Union standing next to
Soviet Premier Nikita Khrushchev in 1962.

From War to Rock 'n Roll

***

On October 14, 1962 American "U2" spy planes brought back evidence to the CIA that several medium-range ballistic missile sites were being erected inside Cuba. Acting on this evidence, President Kennedy decreed the total blockade of all ships going from Russia to Cuba to prevent more offensive weapons from getting through to Castro from the Soviet Union. Kennedy also ordered the Pentagon to get ready a full U.S. Marines invasion force in case it was needed.

Kennedy demanded from the Soviets to stop all shipments of offensive weapons to Cuba and that their missiles be taken out of Cuba. On October 24th, several Russian ships approached the blockade and then but were intercepted by U.S. Navy ships and forced to return to Russia. The United States made the Soviets remove all their Medium Range Intercontinental Ballistic Missiles (MRBMs) from Cuba. In return President Kennedy promised not to invade Cuba again, or allow an invasion of exiles to launch from U.S. soil. The standoff would be known to the world as the October Missile crisis.

However, the Cuban exiles with support from the CIA, continued to harass Cuba by infiltrating spies, saboteurs, and even commando teams to try to assassinate Fidel Castro.

Soviet Medium Range Ballistic Missiles like the ones deployed in
Cuba in 1962

A P2V Neptune US patrol plane flew above a Soviet freighter during
the Cuban missile crisis in 1962

3.

My enlistment in the Cuban Army

Right before the October missile crisis erupted I was living at my mother's house and wishing that I could leave and do something. I was growing bored with my life in the city and decided that I wanted to join the army, an impulsive decision that turned out to be a "huge mistake". I was fifteen-years-old.

Right before I joined the Army, my maternal grandfather Antonio passed away. The government provided our family with two planes to transfer his body from the province of Habana to Oriente, where the funeral would be held. This was one of the saddest times that I can remember ever. I had been very close to my grandfather and always felt a great affection for him.

A few days before my grandfather died, Fidel Castro paid us a visit. He came over to my grandmother's house when he learned of my grandfather's poor health and wanted to see him. Fidel had a great deal of respect for him and for the rest of my family. This would be the first and last time that I saw Fidel Castro close by.

Upon my return from the funeral, I went ahead with my plans and enlisted in the army. While a new law had just been passed that drafted all boys between the ages of sixteen and twenty-seven years old, I went in voluntarily. The 1962 missile crisis had begun to unravel, and I was sent to an anti-aircraft training school to learn to become a specialist in fifty-seven millimeters, and in one hundred-millimeter cannons, which used electronic aim and fire controls.

From War to Rock 'n Roll

With my family at my mother's's funeral in Guantanamo.

This military school was in the outskirts of La Habana at a place called Barbosa. The head of the school was Lieutenant Gomez, a man with experience in war tactics but practically an illiterate. He was very tough on us in our transition from civilians to soldiers and didn't know enough about people and their feelings for doing that kind of work, I thought.

My Grandfather Antonio Rodiles.

All the new recruits were forced to stay at the training camp for the first six months without leave. We had to keep our heads completely shaven, totally bald. This "shaven head" rule wasn't even carried out in the regular army, something limited to this particular school. That was one of the first things that bothered me about the army, for I wasn't used to do anything by force just because someone wanted to feel that he was in charge of my life.

Three months into the training camp and too often disciplined often for not agreeing with or obeying the camp's policies, I was punished by having to dig a trench to hide a Soviet SON-9 radar unit inside, which was as big as a truck. They also locked inside of a big box that served as a jail cell as punishment. That's when I started looking for the first opportunity to escape from that school.

In the army with a few recruits. I'm in the back row
with a broken arm.

I finally got my chance to escape but had to traverse a good twenty miles of rugged country terrain to get back to my mother's house. I was chased half the way by a sergeant who was waving a drawn pistol at me as he ran in mu pursuit. When I explained to my mother why I had left my military unit she told me that I should have sent the word out to her about how they were treating us there. I told her that there was no way for me to get in touch with her from the school. I wasn't authorized to make any phone calls out, or to reach anyone outside of the school by any means. We realized that my escape had made me a deserter.

My mother made an appointment to meet with the Minister of the Armed Forces, Raul Castro, with whom my family had been close since the insurrection days. When my mother explained the situation to Raul, he ordered that I be given a document authorizing me to remain out of the artillery school until our meeting took place.

While waiting for our meeting with Raul Castro, I went to live at my grandmother's house on 1st Avenue between 46th Street and 60th Street in the neighborhood of Miramar. Next door to my grandmother lived the then President of Cuba, Osvaldo Dorticos Torrado.

One day a man named Gomez, the lieutenant in charge at the Barbosa training camp, showed up at my grandmother's house looking for me. The purpose of his visit was to arrest me and take me back to the training camp. When he got to the house he ran into two armed guards on the sidewalk. The guards had been permanently deployed outside her house to protect my two uncles who were high-ranking officers in the Cuban military. The lieutenant was very surprised to see where I lived and approached the house with caution. The guards stopped him before he got to the driveway and asked him of his purpose for being there. The man explained that he had come for me.

One of the guards went into the house to get the document from Raul and show it to lieutenant Gomez. When Gomez read the paper and saw that it was signed by Raul Castro he left without saying a word. Having realized the family he was dealing with, Gomez was definitely worried about the possible repercussion he might have to face for his abusive treatment of the new recruits at the training camp.

The house in Miramar where my grandmother lived was next to president Osvaldo Dorticos' and was kept under heavy armed security twenty-four-seven. There had been a few attempts to assassinate Dorticos and the government wasn't taking any chances. I had personally witnessed one attempt on his life, though at the time I didn't know what was happening.

On that scary night, I was walking back to my grandmother's house at around two o'clock after an evening out playing music with some friends. That's when I suddenly heard a barrage of gunfire nearby. I ran and hid underneath one of the cars in the driveway until the shooting stopped, not knowing what was going on, or who was shooting whom.

Later on, I found out that a team of Cuban commandos from Miami had made an incursion on the island aboard a PT boat with the plan to kill the president. They had opened fired from their boat on what they thought was a library window at Dorticos' house was a light was on every night. They believed he would be inside the library because it was usually the only light that stayed on in his house at night.

Instead, what the attackers had mistakenly aimed at was a light in the city aquarium which was located very close by. The commandos' action was ineffective and just caused the destruction of a few fish tanks at the aquarium. But there was a swift response. As soon as the commandos opened fire on the aquarium from the PT boat, the guards opened fire back from land with their automatic weapons. It was a very frightening moment for me.

A week after, Raul's *aide d 'camp* came for me at my grandmother's house for my much-anticipated meeting with Raul Castro. My mother decided to come along with me to see Raul.

Inside Raul's office, my first words were "I want to be punished for escaping from the training camp because it was the wrong way for me to handle the situation. However, it only way I had to get the information out about the cruel ways of lieutenant Gomez and other officers in the camp."

The only thing I asked of Raul Castro was to order an investigation into the practices at that camp. Raul listened to me and then called an officer into his office and ordered him to carry out the investigation at Barbosa.

Raul then signed my transfer to a fifty-seven-millimeter anti-aircraft base located outside of Havana and not far from a fishing town called Cojimar. He also ordered that I was not to be given any leave passes at all until he personally gave them the authorization to do so. That was Raul's way to punish me for my escape from the Barbosa camp. Later on, I learned that after the Barbosa camp investigation was carried out and lieutenant Gomez and two sergeants were punished for imposing extreme disciplinary measures on the recruits.

I was summoned to the Cuban air and anti-aircraft headquarters located at the Libertad airport, where a commander named Oropesa would escort me to my new unit. In fact, both commander Oropesa and commander Chabeco, the chief at the Libertad air base drove me to the anti-aircraft unit in Cojimar known as the "1225 battery of 57-millimeter cannons".

Soviet-made 57 mm anti-aircraft gun.

At Cojimar, my escorts introduced me to the officer in charge - lieutenant John, a man who had been born in the United States and raised in Cuba. John was about twenty years old and just out of military school which he had attended for three years. He had no combat experience and had not been involved in the insurrection war at all. "This assignment was already getting on my nerves", I thought.

I was also introduced to the sergeant in charge, a guy named Manso. Manso was a short and fat true mother fucker who acted like he was superior to everyone else and enjoyed abusing his powers at random. Once commanders Oropesa and Chabeco left, I started to feel trapped again. It was Barbosa *redux* all over.

Lieutenant Johnny, as the people there called John, ordered sergeant Manso to take me to my barracks and assign me a bunk bed. Manso briefed me on what I had to do if the alarm was sounded in the unit. I was told to go immediately to AA battery number five, stand by it and wait for orders from my squad corporal.

That night, I met the other soldiers at the unit and told them that I had been transferred from the Barbosa camp, but avoided given any details of the reason for my relocation. They all assumed that the reason the unit was ordered no to give me leaves was because of some ordinary disciplinary reason. They didn't know that I had actually gone AWOL from Barbosa.

The next day started at five o'clock in the morning, when we were ordered to get out of bed and go into formation outside for the daily activities. During the day, we had to attend academic classes of high school level and on anti-aircraft machine guns. We had drills almost every day of the week to maintain our state of readiness for an attack. The Soviet AA cannons that we handled were guided by radar and a fire director. Those devices provided the canons with the calculations for altitude and distance through electronic conductors. There were two electric plants at the camp to provide the power needed to operate to the anti-aircraft equipment.

A few of us would spend our free time at camp playing music, and most of my friends in that group were black Cubans. The type of music we played in those days was called "guaguancó", a typical afro-Cuban music that had a very happy and contagious rhythm to it. Those were indeed my most memorable times in the army.

Spy ship USS Oxford anchored outside Cuban international waters during the missile crisis.

In the afternoons, we could see clearly the American battle-ship USS Oxford anchored in international waters off the coast of Cuba at about three o'clock from our base. It was still close enough that we could see the ship in detail. The USS Oxford was a spy ship with the specific mission to watch the island and eaves-drop on its military communications. Often, we also watched as P2B Neptune planes flew over and around the ship. Sometimes the planes would cross over the border of international waters into Cuban waters, which made us scramble to get our defenses ready against a possible attack.

A good five months went by when our unit received the orders to move to a different location. It was five in the afternoon when we were given the orders to pack our belongings and prepare to abandon camp. Only seven soldiers would stay behind to guard the large ammunitions depot. When hooked the AA cannons to the truck hitches, put the tarpaulin covers on them, lined up our nine trucks on the road and were ready to go. None of us had the vaguest idea where we were going to, only the officers knew the location of our new deployment.

We left Cojimar at eight o'clock at night and after driving for three hours we arrived at an area in the back of a military airport known as San Antonio de los Baños. We started to unload our trucks, emplace the cannons set up our new camp. It had started to rain when we got there, making it difficult to find hard ground where to set up the cannons. A security perimeter was established, and armed guards were placed in all the surrounding areas. That when we realized we had to find our own places to sleep in the open since we had not brought ant tents with us.

That night, we slept outdoors. I managed to find the scabbard of a palm leaf to use as a cover for my hammock which I had hung between two trees. My idea failed when the wind blew off the scabbard away forcing me to spend the entire night getting soaked by the rain, just like everyone else.

The next day things got better organized and we started to become familiar with the area. I found out that were deployed next to a surface to air missile unit – SAM - the place we were supposed to guard.

Our unit, in turn, was protected by an emplacement of thirty-seven-millimeter anti-aircraft cannons outside our perimeter. On this second day in the new camp a truck came to deliver three canvas tents. Along with the truck came a Jeep with the captain of the SAM unit, who wanted to pass inspection of our entire unit. Meanwhile, we had already set up the tents and dug trenches to protect our cannons. The area around us had a lot of vegetation, so we had plenty of natural camouflage to use for our camp.

While the captain was there we underwent a sudden practice drill. When the alarm sounded, I thought to myself, "now it's time to show this captain what we've got."

It took us less than one minute to uncover all the cannons and get them ready to be fired. Our defenses were ready. There was a competition going on between the different units to see which unit could do the drill in the shortest time, and records were kept for all the units. We were very proud of our readiness capabilities and of our performance on that day.

Soon, our lives became again a routine the same as in Cojimar. After a whole month, I still have not gotten any passes authorizing me to leave the camp. I believed that my punishment had been way too harsh and was very angry for having to stay in the camp while my fellow soldiers left regularly to visit their families. My father had come and see me a few times, but he didn't use his influence to help me get a leave because he felt that I should complete my punishment, something that was arbitrarily in the hands of Raul Castro. Meanwhile, sergeant Manso, who had been transferred with us had been abusing his power over us more and more each day that went by.

Our unit was made up of older soldiers with seven to eight years of army experience and the rest were recruits, therefore there were many differences between those two groups. However, every night we all got together to dance and play guagauancó music.

One night while on guard duty next to a radar unit, I sat down, hidden behind a bush and fell asleep. It was around four o'clock in the morning and I was very tired from all the work that day, but my sleep was always light, and I woke up upon hearing footsteps heading my way. It was sergeant Manso.

I knew that Manso had been making rounds every night around the radar unit trying to catch us asleep while on duty. Instead, it was me who surprised him. I was armed with a B-2 Czech rifle with bayonet that flicked out with a sharp movement of the gun. When Manso walked by the bush where I was laying, I jumped out at him, flicked the bayonet in a second and pointed it at his throat. The sergeant turned white and almost fainted before my eyes, as I began to apologize and explained that I had seen his shadow and was just checking to see who he was. I don't remember ever laughing so hard after he left.

Manso and I clashed in another occasion when he came into the barracks at three o'clock in the morning and ordered me to get up and take a shower. He did this to me as a punishment for almost starting a fight that day. I went ahead and took a freezing cold shower since it was very cold outside, and there was no water heater. During my whole deployment at San Antonio de los Baños, sergeant Manso and I continued to have disagreements, but he always had the upper hand since he was a sergeant.

I started taking high-school classes outside the camp, which gave me a break from my punishment of not having authorized leaves. This was my first contact with the outside world since I arrived at that unit.

Before this, the teachers had come to the camp, but it was too far for them to come all the time. While at school, I made friends with Julia, a girl who was in most of my classes. After a few days into our friendship, I asked Julia to come and sneak into the camp to the place where my friend and I would be on guard duty that night. My friend came and brought along a girlfriend along, who was supposed to spend time with my friend Macau. Macau has gotten his nickname because of the resemblance to a sea creature that bore that name.

Right away, my girlfriend's friend reacted to Macau's odd looks and refuse to be with him. Julia and I went into the woods while Macau and the other girl stayed back to watch for Sergeant Manso. From the woods, we heard Julia's friend screaming and we ran out to see what happened. We found out that she was very upset over Macau trying to touch her. He told me later that he lost control after not having been with a girl for a very long time.

My relationship with Julia didn't last long because once again I received the orders that we were to be transferred to Oriente after spending five months in San Antonio de los Baños. While the recruits were to stay there, the older soldiers were sent to Oriente where their families lived. As a continuation of my punishment, I was ordered to go to Oriente with the older soldiers. I hadn't expected to be forced to move there since my family lived in Habana, not in Oriente. Then I got even worse news. Sergeant Manso would be going along with us to Oriente.

We packed everything and then drove to a military cargo railroad station where we loaded all our equipment onto a train. There were two lieutenants and one other sergeant in charge besides Manso.

We boarded the train and departed from the station at around ten o'clock at night. We passed many small towns, where the people would come out and cheer us on. We took turns riding on top of the cars to guard the train and during our fourth day trip to Oriente we went through several rain showers and we got soaked to our core. That trip was indeed very uncomfortable. When we arrived at a station at six o'clock in the morning we saw a sign at the station reading *Holguin, Oriente.* There were several officers from a nearby Air Force Base called *Base Aerea de Holguin* waiting for us at the station. This was the largest air base on the entire island. When I found out where we were going I got excited because I had always been interested in flying. If I could not spend my life playing music, then I had hoped to someday become a pilot.

We were taken to the air force base and set-up our unit at the end of the runway, hidden inside of a tree forest. We were only about five-hundred feet away from the runway and I enjoyed watching the planes take off, do their flight exercises and then land. While I was at that base I developed a true passion for flying.

***

At the base I met a sergeant who was a flight instructor. He owned a motorcycle and one day I saw that he was having trouble fixing it. I offered to help him since I had grown up with motorcycles and knew a lot about them. After I helped him fix his bike we became good friends and viewed each other as equals, not as an officer and a subordinate.

Often, in my spare time, I would sit in on his classes at the flying school and one day he offered to take me up for a ride on a jet fighter. I accepted without hesitation. The plane he took me up for a brief flight over Oriente was a two-seater, Soviet-made MIG-15 used specifically for training. After that flight, I had my mind made up to apply for flying school at the first opportunity.

MIG-15 UTI trainer similar to the one I flew as a passenger in Holguin, Cuba.

Not long after that, an officer brought applications for flight school for us recruits to fill out. Anyone who believed had all the physical and mental requirements could apply. To become a pilot, the candidates had to be between the ages of sixteen and twenty-four, couldn't wear vision corrective glasses, and had to meet many other physical requirements. Only three men from my unit filled out applications. We were to go to the military hospital near the Libertad Air Base in La Habana to take our physical exams.

Before   we left the Holguin Air Base we took a pre-physical examination along with all the flight candidates from other units had also signed up. There were about a thousand of us in total, but only two hundred were accepted to move on after the two-day pre-physical tests. The two other guys from my unit did not pass, and I was sent to La Habana to undergo the strenuous MIG jet fighter physical test at the military hospital.

On the day of our pre-physical tests, an unfortunate accident occurred at air base. A MIG-15 on a routine flight crashed and the pilot got killed. The pilot had been ordered to jump from the plane when the engine began to have trouble, but the pilot refused to leave the plane. A similar accident had happened to another pilot before, but he had jumped, and the plane was destroyed. Apparently, this pilot though he could save the plane and paid for his mistake with his life. When we went to look at the plane on the ground after the crash we found only burnt remains of the plane and the pilot's body. This incident frightened me to a certain extent, but I still wanted to learn to fly.

The two-hundred of us who had passed the first physical tests were put on buses to travel to La Habana. We were first taken to Libertad Air Base, where we were to stay until it was time to start the tests at the nearby hospital. There were many recruits from other units waiting there also. By applying to the air force, I had managed to find a a way out of having to complete my punishment. Nobody had caught on to that as yet.

However, that didn't last long. While at t Libertad, I ran into commander Oropesa, the chief of the anti-aircraft forces who asked me what I was doing there. I told him that I was waiting to take tests for the flight school and all he said to me then was that "he'd look into it."

We eventually started physical tests, which took a total of six days to complete. I passed them all along with eleven others who had come with my group of two hundred from Holguin. We were supposed to be going to the air force school at the San Julian base in the province of Pinar del Rio.

The day before we were supposed to leave for San Julian, I was summoned to the office of commander Oropesa. Also waiting for me there was commander Chabeco, the head of the Cuban Air Force at the time. They told me that that because of my disciplinary records from the army, they decided that I would have to spend two more years in the anti-aircraft forces before I could join the air force.

I told them that I didn't want to go back to Holguin. While I had already spent two and a half years in the army, Chabeco didn't give me much of an alternative. I was given the choice to go back to the anti-aircraft unit in Holguin for two more years, or spend my time left in the army cutting sugar cane in the fields. I thought that the chances of me passing the tests again in two years was very unlikely, so I decided to cut sugar cane instead, get out of the army altogether and give up my dream of becoming a pilot. I felt cheated once again, but I couldn't do anything about it.

I was immediately sent to a sugar cane camp in the province of Matanzas. There, we had to get up every morning at five o'clock to start work by seven o'clock, working straight through to six o'clock at night with just one small break at noon for lunch. I despised every single minute spent there; it was the hardest work I had ever done in my life and also the most boring. Being forced to work by military officers made it much harder for me to endure. I had someone still ordering me around all the time. My only relief while at the sugar cane camp was getting together with other guys to play music at night. We put together a small good group of musicians that eventually got leaves from our camp to visit other camps and offer them entertainment. It was there and then when I reaffirmed my decision to spend my life playing music.

One night, five of us decided to sneak out of our camp and attend a dance that was being held only a few towns away from where we were located. While we realized that if we were caught doing this, our punishment would be severe. But the hard work that we were doing in the fields made us feel entitled to go out and have a good time.

That night, we left the camp at dusk and walked for at least five miles to get to the main highway where we could hitch a ride into the town where the dance was going to take place. We stayed at the party until very late and didn't get back to the camp until four in the morning, with barely half hour of sleep or so before it was time to get up and go to work. When I jumped into my bed I found that some of the guys had played a bad joke on me. I had laid on a bed covered with sugar and water.

Time passed very slow in the camp, but I finally got my release papers arrived after having spent three years of my life in the army. I was finally free, at least from having to take orders from the army imbecile officers, from the harsh discipline, and the inhumane working conditions at the sugar cane camps. In all, I could not be happier with my newly regained freedom.

4.

Traveling with the Merchant Marine Corps.

I returned to La Habana with no desire of working for a long time. I just wanted to take time off to enjoy my freedom. At that time, the transportation in Cuba was becoming very difficult because to the gasoline-rationing program. I could only buy eight gallons of gasoline every month for our Volkswagen Beetle, so I decided to put together a small motorcycle that I could use to get around since it consumed much less gas than the VW. I went to the beach just about every day and to parties on weekends, just having a plain good time.

Some of my friends who were musicians offered me a gig and we started performing at hospitals and schools for free. I played congas and timbales. I didn't like this gig at all because they forced me to hold a day paying job while playing with the band. There was no professional music in Cuba, therefore I knew that I wasn't going to be able to make my living from music, at least not there. I wanted to travel and visit other places outside Cuba, but the communist regime didn't allow the Cuban people to travel at will. I realized that I didn't want to stay by force on that island for the rest of my life and begun to think of ways to get out of there for good.

In those days I met a girl named, Maria Paz Espejo, who had been born in Chile. Her mother was a psychology teacher and a political refugee from Chile. I spent a lot of time with Maria and soon we fell in love. During my visits to her house, her mother and I would sit and talk for hours and, as usual, our conversation would turn into a political discussion. Although she was very intelligent, I did not agree with some of her ideas. One night while at her house, we received the unexpected visit from Ernesto Ché

Guevara, who was a good friend of Maria's mother. In another occasion, I had the chance to meet Salvador Allende, the former President of Chile there. However, nobody ever knew of my secret intentions to escape from Cuba.

As time passed, Maria and I spent almost all our time together, going skin diving and hanging out at parties. There was a small ocean beach a few blocks away from my house where all our friends usually hung out. It was known as *"la playita de 16"*.

I was then living at my mother's house on 8th Street in Miramar and got bored again after a few months of living that care free, easy life while being pestered by my mother's insistence that I did something productive with my life. While reading the newspaper one day, an article caught my attention. The merchant marine corps was looking to train sailors and machinists who had already spent their time in the army and could go straight to sailor school.

The only requirements to join was to have a high school diploma, had completed three years in the army, and have no family members with an anti-communist background. I was accepted right away thanks to the help from my father, now a commander in the Cuban army. I knew that joining the merchant marines would put me back into a semi-military lifestyle, something that I didn't want at all, but I saw it as my only way out of Cuba. This was my biggest secret ever, even with my family and my close friends. If I played my cards right, I might have the opportunity to escape in a free country and eventually pursue my music career in the USA.

The Naval Academy was located in the Bay of Mariel about an hour drive from La Habana. On the first day I had head shaven and felt like I had joined the army all over again. Even though the merchant marines were a civilian corps, the school at the Naval Academy was attended by both the Cuban Navy recruits and the merchant marine's sailors. If I managed to maintain a good discipline record while at school and didn't get any demerits, I could leave for home on weekends and have my Saturdays and Sundays free.

I spent my weekends with Maria going to the beach and to parties or just be with one another. Six months after I had begun the course, I hurt my leg and was unable to finish. Because of this unfortunate episode, I applied to a civilian course outside the academy, but which was connected to it and offered the same courses.

The theory courses were held at a department of the Transportation Ministry called the Mambisa Navigation Lines. This department had control of the whole Cuban Merchants Marine Corps. The practical courses on the engines and the mechanics of the ships were held at a dry dock in the Bay of La Habana, at a place called Casablanca. The people taking this course were all members of the communist party, which was a requirement of entering the academy. I managed to have the political affiliation requirement wavered because my family's background in the armed insurrection against Batista, and because of my injury that prevented me from completing the school at the Bay of Mariel academy. Now I could make use of my motorcycle to commute back and forth from school and thus avoid having to take the packed and unreliable buses from the public transportation system. But most important, it was great to be out of the military regiment again.

Our first classes were mostly about steam engines, and an introduction to the merchant marine's life in general. After about a month and a half into the course, we were assigned individually to a ship that was docked at the port of Havana. There we were to be taught by sailors and machinists with many years of experience. After a while, I was assigned to a different ship and put in charge of the whole night shift. The type of steam ships that were specializing in had to keep one of the boilers running all night long to maintain the steam generator and provide electrical power. One of the worst things about working on the ship was the intense heat inside the engine room, the place where I would spend most of my time while at sea since I was training to become an engineer.

I passed the first tests on steam room machinery with all A's. I wasn't too interested in the subject but had lots of previous knowledge about engines from my past life. I knew that my first trip on a ship was getting close because two of my classmates were already sailing on a ship that was travelling to Canada. While Maria wasn't too happy over the idea of me being gone for months at a time, I couldn't be more thrilled of finally getting underway.

My family was very happy that I had joined the corps and taken the initiative to do something with my life. The time that I had been waiting for finally came and I was all set to go. I got assigned to work on a steam ship called "Bahia Santiago de Cuba" which was consigned to make a delivery in Europe. It was time to say goodbye to Maria and have her accept the fact that I would be gone for several months.

Our first trip would be to Las Palmas in the Canary Islands. Our ship, built in 1944, was a three thousand ton, 258 feet long aging American steamship equipped with two boilers and a steam engine positioned in the middle of the ship. There was a tunnel going from the center of the hull, where the engine was, to the stern where the propeller axel ran through. This tunnel was also used by the sailors to get from one place to another during bad weather, when it was too dangerous to walk on the deck and risk getting washed overboard by a wave. The crew consisted of thirty-four men, with my cabin located along with three others at the stern of the ship. Each cabin had enough room for just three men. The rest of the cabins were in the middle part of the ship near the engine and the bridge. There were two storage bays for the merchandise we carried, one was between the center and the stern of the ship and the other was between the bow and the center of the ship.

Cargo ship Bahia Santiago de Cuba.

On the first night after we left, the ocean was very rough, and we almost didn't make it out of La Habana harbor. I felt sick during the beginning of the trip but by morning I was feeling much better although the ocean was still very choppy. At lunchtime I learned that I wasn't the only one of the crew who got a little sick. As the day passed, everyone gradually became more adjusted to the ship's movement. At night, we all gathered in the dining room to play cards, dominos or whatever we wanted to do. Many of us spent our leisure time playing music since there were a few instruments on board, mostly percussion instruments, timbales, congas, cowbells and even a few guitars. I had arrived, I thought. Being on that ship with all the open water around also gave me a feeling of freedom that I had never felt before.

I began my work shift on the first day at four o'clock in the morning until seven in the morning and then again from four in the afternoon until seven o'clock at night. My time was divided with this six-hour break so that I could get out of the intense heat in the engine room where I worked. We also had to attend classes for three hours every afternoon during our break. My job on the ship consisted of keeping the water level and the pressure in the boilers at the right level to supply the engine with steam.

On the fourth day of our trip we were entering an area called *the Sargasso Sea* in the Atlantic Ocean, where I saw first-hand the endless patches of *Sargassum* seaweed floating on top of the ocean. The Sargasso Sea is also the home of a great variety of marine life, and the migration destination of sharks, whales and eels.

One of the things that impressed me the most during this trip was the capture of a giant sailfish by an old Spanish sailor known as Cordal. I enjoyed sitting down and talking with Cordal because the great knowledge he had gathered throughout his many years at sea - the man had spent the past thirteen years aboard the same ship. Next to my cabin lived another sailor named Portuondo, who was in charge of keeping all of the engine's parts lubricated while the engine was running. On the seventh night of our trip as we left the Sargasso Sea the ocean started to get rough again. That night while I was on my way to my work shift through the tunnel I noticed that Portuondo was late. When he finally came in, he was soaking wet and told us that he tried to cross the ship over the deck and had miscalculated a wave that almost washed him overboard hadn't he not grabbed onto a pole to keep himself anchored on board. Later that night, Portuondo began to tell me a lot about the ship that I hadn't known before. He showed me many holes on the bottom of the ship that had been filled in with cement. What I saw made me wonder if we were safe on that ship.

On our tenth day at sea we heard over our radio that we were heading into a very bad storm. As we sailed farther on, the ocean turned rougher and the waves started bouncing our small ship all over the place. It began to thunder, and the waves were washing right over the ship. The ship was going under the waves and coming out on the other side. The 258 feet long *Bahia de*

Santiago de Cuba, which had seemed big to me before, was being tossed around like a piece of fragile paper by the wind and the huge waves. I was scared while on my work shift, sliding all over while the boat was being thrown from side to side, almost to the point of being pushed completely over. I kept a close eye on the instrument that shows with a needle when the boat is being turned too far by the waves and about to capsize.

The next morning, we noticed that we had been losing our supply of fresh water. There was a leak in the tanks somewhere and some of the potable water tanks were already empty. We didn't have a water purifier on the ship and so whatever we held onboard was indeed vital to our survival. The ship also needed this water to run the steam engine and without the engine running the captain could not steer the ship and we would surely capsize. So far, the captain had been maneuvering the ship skillfully through the waves at the right angle so as not to be turned over.

We sent out a S.O.S. signal of distress to try and get some water from another ship in the area if there were any ships close by. We heard over the radio that a Greek ship had caught on fire. While this ship was very close to us we couldn't stop to help them because we had to fix our own problem, or our entire crew could perish. We tried searching for the leak in the tanks but, couldn't find it and the rough ocean made it impossible for anyone to dive under water and check the outside of the tanks.

We did receive an answer to our S.O.S. from another Cuban ship, a fourteen thousand ton, Japanese made ship that was very new, well equipped, and was faring alright in the storm. They responded that they were going to try and get close enough to us to help. As the Conrado Benitez got close to us, we prepare to receive a rope shot by them with a rope gun, a flare type gun that shot out a rope instead of a flare. Once we had their rope, we managed to send a hose over so they could transfer the water to us.

Within seconds after we connected the hose to our ship it snapped in half as the two ships got thrown apart by a wave. After this had failed we tried a different size rope that a big ship would use to dock alongside us. This rope also broke within minutes. That was very scary because it was our last chance to get help from the *Conrado Benitez* and our water supply was running out fast. The few times that I ran into the ship's chief engineer the man seemed very nervous about our situation and he admitted to me that this was one of the worse storms he had ever been through. The storm was too strong, and he didn't think the ship was well equipped enough to handle the it. We tried everything that we could think of to solve this crisis but, the night passed, and none of our ideas worked out. Everyone knew that if the storm didn't subside within the next twenty-four hours we were doomed for disaster.

We heard that the Greek ship that had caught fire earlier had sunk and that there had been no survivors. The waves had been too large for any ship to get close to help in what was reported as a force 7 gale. By morning, it started to rain. Meanwhile, the storm was growing stronger as our water supply dwindled very fast. We gathered all the canvass that we had on board and spread them out on deck to catch every drop of rain water possible and then funnel it to the water tanks using the hoses. We managed to keep the engine running in a move that actually saved us from sinking. Finally, by nine o'clock at night the ocean had calmed down enough for us to get another hose from our ship to the *Conrado Benitez,* which had remained sailing nearby during the storm. The next day, the crisis was over. However, we heard on the radio some very bad news. Four other ships besides the Greek ship had sunk in the same area where we had been. Those ships had been bigger and better equipped than our ship. We had gotten through that killer storm mostly on good luck.

As we approached the Strait of Gibraltar, the sky had cleared considerably, and the seas had mellowed out. Once we passed through the strait, we knew that the danger was over, and that we would make it to Las Palmas. I was amazed at the sight of Africa on the right side of the ship, and Spain on the other. There was the impressive English protectorate known as the "Rock of Gibraltar" on the Spanish side looking like a huge-chested woman against the Mediterranean skies. There were dolphins, hundreds of them, popping out of the water all around our ship. On the fourteenth day of our journey we finally arrived in Las Palmas in the Canary Islands.

It was New Year's Eve and we had arrived just before midnight. However, we had to wait outside of the entrance to the bay until the boat from the port authority could come and to lead us into the bay. After waiting for a while we were guided in and dropped anchor in the middle of the bay. From our position we could hear the sounds of the New Year's celebrations and loud music playing everywhere. By order of the Spanish government, we were not allowed to get off the ship after nine o'clock at night, so we had no choice but to lay back and listen to the sounds of the celebrations.

The Spanish government curfew had to do with the fact that our ship was from a communist country. All other ships from the communist block were also subject to the curfew. The next day we got authorization to dock at Las Palmas. As we proceeded to the dock we saw a huge crowd of onlookers staring at our old ship, which had been damaged by the storm and listing to one side. As we docked, an old sailor said "if there is a God, he is a sailor and Cuban" after he heard the stories about our journey and seeing the condition of our ship.

The much-needed ship repairs began right away but we were told that it would take at least seven days to find and fix the leaks in the water tanks. The engine also needed general repairs and there were other minor damages that had to be taken care of before we could set sail again. In Las Palmas, the crew was handed an amount of money in U.S. dollars to be spent as we pleased.

Most of the men spent their money on clothing articles that couldn't be bought in Cuba, like nylon shirts, blue jeans and shoes.

Others spent their money on gifts to bring back to their families, and on wine. After we unloaded our cargo destined for Las Palmas, which represented half of our load, and once all the repairs were taken care of, we left to make the remaining of our cement cargo, first to Cartagena and the rest to Set, in France. We stayed in Set for a few days, where I visited a few night clubs and watched several rock bands performing. Rock 'n Roll was illegal in Cuba and ironically it was my passion. I enjoyed my trip to Europe, witnessing first-hand how democratic societies lived and functioned, and learning about different people and cultures.

From France, we went back to Las Palmas to refuel the ship for the trip back to Cuba. On that day, we went again through another very bad storm. I was more familiar with the ocean by then and the inclement weather didn't bother me too much. We stayed in Las Palmas for another five days while more repairs were being made on the ship. On our journey back to Cuba we made a final stop in Agadir, Morocco to pick up a load of fertilizer to take back to the island.

Morocco was a much different experience for me because of the way the people had adapted to the desert life and developed their own culture. The Moroccans were indeed very strange people to me. Everyone was dressed in long and heavy robes and married women wore veils to cover their faces in a display of respect. While I was in a bar having a beer with other sailors, a drunken Greek sailor molested a woman that had a veil over here face, which was a huge offence in that country. The Greek sailor was later found dead.

While in Morocco I met an Argentinean artist who was traveling around the country with his wife and daughter in a Volkswagen bus. He taught me a little bit about the art of molding copper, so I nicknamed him the "copper man". I went several times to the camping grounds where he and his family were staying, and where we talked a lot about different places and politics. This camp was a safe place because it had armed guards protecting it. Copper man warned me that Morocco was a place filled with thieves who would hit anyone who dared to walk on the streets late at night. The "copper man" and me played some music together also and made me feel lucky to have found some-one to help me get by in that strange country.

In Agadir, we eventually loaded the ship's cargo hold half the way with fertilizer and steamed back to Cuba, skimming the coast of Africa for as far as we could. The Atlantic Ocean was surprisingly calm this time around which made the voyage ra-ther enjoyable. After entering the waters of the Gulf of Mexico, I was lying on the deck when I suddenly heard a loud splash in the water right next to the ship. I looked over and saw a big black wale blowing water through the hole in top of his head as he jumped out of the water. Everyone on the ship came out to watch this giant creature, for it was a very rare occurrence to spot a whale in the warm waters of the Gulf of Mexico. Three days later, on a very dark night, I saw the lighthouse at the Morro Castle at the entrance of the Havana Bay. We headed straight for the light.

Morro Castle and lighthouse, entrance to the Bay of Havana.

Our ship had to wait a few hours at the entrance of the harbor a space to dock and unload the cargo. Several boats eventually came to pick us up and bring us to land. I was one of the first to leave the ship.

My family was very happy to see me returning safe and sound and everyone went crazy with the gifts that I had brought back for them. The next day I went to see Maria and brought her gift. That night we went to a party together and I saw a good friend of mine there, Frank, who told me that his parents had left Cuba and left their house for him to keep. It was a huge house with an indoor swimming pool. Frank offered to let me live in half of his house and I accepted gladly. Frank's girlfriend Cristina and Maria came almost every night to our house to party. But soon enough I learned that my ship had been consigned to make another trip, this time to deliver cement to the island of Martinique and pick up a cargo of potato seeds to bring back to Cuba.

From War to Rock 'n Roll

I found the island of Martinique populated mostly by French speaking, cheerful black people. There was music coming out of every open window and doorway. As we got ready to dock in Martinique our ship hit an underwater piling which caused a large dent on the hull that had to be repaired. It was an expensive repair, about nine hundred dollars we were told, and there would be an investigation to find out who had been responsible for the accident. While we stayed docked on the island, the crew of a Spanish ship that was docked next to us invited us to join them at a party on their ship. We agreed to go and brought our music instruments to play for them.

We spent seven days in Martinique before returning to Cuba. We were headed straight for the port of Cienfuegos to unload the potato seeds cargo that we had brought with us. On the way to Cienfuegos, a piece of lumber fell on my foot and broke my toe and tore off half of my toenail. Since there were no medical supplies on our ship to treat my injury, I had to wait until we got to Cienfuegos to receive medical treatment. By the time we arrived in Cienfuegos my foot had become badly infected and I was sent to Havana directly by bus after being treated at a local hospital.

5.

My Escape from Cuba

After completing my first two voyages on a Cuban merchant marine ship I realized that my escape from the island was long overdue. I returned to Havana and went to the *Terminales Mambisas* headquarters where I got a month's leave to recover from my foot injury. Everything seemed to be going smoothly for me until I had to break up with Maria. I found out that she'd been having a relationship with Frank and went crazy with anger. I went to the house right away and moved all my things out. Meanwhile, a friend named Bode offered me a place to stay at his home.

I decided to go after Frank's girlfriend, Christina, at first just out of revenge. Christina and I started dating and after a short while we realized that we got along very well. I saw that Frank was very hurt by our relationship, something that gave me a great deal of satisfaction. A few weeks, later Christina and I decided to get married. I was nineteen years old and all I had in mind in those days was to materialize my escape from Cuba. I entrusted Christina with my plans and told her that once I was settled in the USA I would arrange for her to join me there. She agreed. Christina and I got married a few weeks later and I was assigned to make another trip on the *Bahia de Santiago de Cuba*, this time to Canada.

As soon as I learned of our new destination I knew that would the perfect opportunity for me to escape and try to cross over to the USA. On the day I left for Canada a friend called Rafael Ferrer gave me a ride on my motorcycle to where the ship was docked. Christina also showed up to say goodbye. She was the only one who knew what I was up to.

We departed from Havana and headed up towards Canada

through an area known as the Devils Triangle. On our way there I could see the coast of Miami in the distance. I was tempted to grab a mask and fins and jump overboard to swim to shore, but the water was way too rough and the shore was at least three miles away. While I didn't know what our situation in Canada would be, I decided to wait until then to try and abandon ship.

In my mind, Miami was the place I wanted to end up at because I have heard of the many opportunities that existed there to grow as a professional musician. Although I was bilingual, it would be also much easier for me to adjust to the American way of life in a place where most people spoke Spanish.

Our port of destination in Canada was Prince Edwards Island. When we arrived, I was off duty and decided to leave the ship right away. I was very nervous as I walked alone away from the dock. I didn't know where to go so I just roamed around the area for a while until I came across a police station. It was time to make my move.

I walked inside the police station where I told the officer on duty that I had just deserted from my ship and was seeking political asylum from the government of Canada. I told them that I couldn't return to Cuba because they would put me in jail.

The officer at the station didn't know how to deal with my case and told me that he would have to contact the immigration authorities on my behalf. For my own protection, I was held overnight in a cell at the police station. I was nervous but realized that I had no choice but to trust those people. I had already made the radical move to set myself free from the Cuban regime and was determined to see it through all the way.

In the morning, another Canadian officer picked-me up from the station and drove me to the airport, which was about three miles away. After the drive to the airport that seemed to take forever, I boarded a flight to Halifax that had been pre-arranged for me. I didn't think of myself as a deserter because I had already given much of my life to my country, but a refuge from a communist regime that had betrayed me and my family. I thought of myself more like a "citizen of the world" who shouldn't be prohibited from traveling anywhere.

From the airport in Halifax I was taken to the immigration center located near the Port of Halifax where I had to fill out the official forms for my petition for asylum in Canada. I was assigned a bed in a room with four other refugees; two men from East Germany, one from Bulgaria and one from Czechoslovakia. None of us spoke a common language therefore we could not communicate with one another, however we still tried to make sense using an improvised form sign language.

I was told that I would be staying there while I went through the legal processing and debriefing. A few times a day for seven days I was taken into an office for questioning by the Canadian immigration officers. Once they learned about my family background they offered to return me to the ship and make it look as if I have had an accident. The Canadians wanted me to go back to Cuba and work as a spy for their government. I refused. I told them that I had escaped to my freedom mostly because I wanted to play music and definitely didn't want to get involved with politics or become a secret agent in Cuba.

When the Canadian immigration police finished the debriefings, they gave me back my identification papers, my Cuban passport, and everything else that they had taken except for a newspaper article that showed a picture of me together with Raul Castro.

During all the days that followed I was still confined to the detention center, but now I could leave the building from three in the afternoon until nine o' clock at night.

While in Halifax I visited the American Consulate and made an appointment with the Consul to discuss the possibility of my getting a visa to enter the United States. On the day of my appointment, I was given a visa application to fill out. I was also told that to get a visa I must have either a place to reside in the

United States and a contract of employment or have family there willing to support me financially after my arrival. If I met those requirements I would still have to wait 90 days or more for the visa to be cleared by the U.S. Government.

I could not meet any of those requirements and wasn't going to wait for 90 days just to hear the decision that my visa had been denied. After that attempt, I understood that I didn't have much of a chance to enter the USA legally. And I did not want to stay in Canada either – I didn't feel like I could have a music future there.

One afternoon while at the immigration center, I received a visit by Father Macho, a Spanish priest who had worked in Cuba for many years. We got along well and decided to get together. We met for lunch at a restaurant in a big hotel where he introduced me to the restaurant's manager. Father Macho wanted to help me get a job at the restaurant, so I could have some money of my own.

Fernando, the restaurant's manager offered me a job as a dishwasher. After getting a tour of the kitchen and seeing the big machines that did all the dishwashing I figured that the job was a piece of cake and accepted without hesitation. I needed to make some money to survive while I figured out what to do next.

The next morning, I arrived for work very early and started doing the breakfast dishes. There were piles and piles of dishes and I soon found out that job wasn't as easy as it had appeared the day before. The dirty dishes just kept pouring into the kitchen for me to load in and out of the washer. By night time, I was overwhelmed by the many dirty dishes from dinner and knew then that I wasn't going to be able to handle the job. I quit the very next day.

I went back to see father Macho and learned from him about other Cubans who had attempted to cross the border with the United States illegally and didn't make it. I asked him why people would try to get into the U.S. without authorization papers.

What would happen then? He told me of an unwritten law that stated that if a Cuban national was caught in the USA after having crossed over the border illegally, he or she would be allowed to remain in the United States. The reason was mainly because the Canadian government would not accept the refuge back and the U.S. government would never send him or her back to Cuba where they would inevitably end up in prison.

That day, Father Macho and I sat talking for a long time. He was anxious to hear all about how Cuba was in those days since he had not had the opportunity to meet many Cubans fresh out of the country.

As soon as I heard about this "unwritten law", I decided to give it a try and started thinking for ways to cross over to the USA illegally. On my way back to the immigration center from my meeting with Father Macho I stopped at a store to buy a compass and a map of the American–Canadian border. I wanted to study the map to find an adequate spot from where to cross into the States.

On the next day, the other guys at the detention center told me were going out for a while and ask me to join them but, I said that I felt like staying in for the day. That morning I received a money order for two hundred dollars that Cristina's father had sent me from Florida.

After the other guys left, I gathered as many clothes as I could, mostly jackets and sweaters, and bundled them inside a nylon jacket. It was the middle of the autumn season and was very cold for me for I was not used to the frigid Canadian weather. I headed straight for the bus station to board a bus for St. Stephens, the nearest city from Halifax to the U.S. border. The bus's first stop was in St. John, where we were told that there would be a delay.

While I was waiting in St. John for the bus to resume the journey I went out for a walk and stepped into a store where. To my surprise, I suddenly spotted there three Cuban sailors from another ship whom I knew. I turned around and ran out of the tore before they could even see me. Had they spotted me they could have tried to force me back to their ship and taken me back to Cuba.

I went back to the bus terminal and hid inside the bathroom to avoid being seen by anyone who might have any reason to stop me. I remained hiding in the bathroom until about nine o' clock when my bus eventually left St. John on its way to St. Stephens.

We arrived in St. Stephens by one o' clock in the morning. It was a small bus terminal with an empty room and a few benches typical of a very small town. From the terminal building I could see the bridge that connected the town of St. Stephens to the town of Calais in the State of Main in the USA. The body of water that separated the two cities was the St. John river, which has begun to freeze.

There were guards posted on both sides of the bridge, which I assumed would be there all day and night. It was October 14, 1969. I wasn't sure on how I would go about to cross the border, only that I had to do it. I walked out of the bus station and began to follow the street that ran parallel to the St. John River to find a spot to cross it at. It was nighttime and all the houses in the city were dark and the streets were deserted.

I had followed the road by the river for about fifteen minutes when I saw the lights of a car and noticed that it was a police cruiser. They stopped to question me. I told them that I was a Cuban sailor looking for a hotel to spend the night in because I was to meet some relatives the next day that were crossing over from the U.S. to see me. The officers offered to take me to a hotel and even brought me inside, as to make sure that I booked a room there. I thank the officers for their help. Once in my room I laid down to rest for a while because I knew that very soon I would have to be on the run once the immigration agents in Halifax noticed that I had not returned to the detention center. I expected the Canadian authorities to start looking all over for me as early as the next day.

After taking an hour and a half nap I went downstairs to the lobby ready to leave but found the front door locked. I called the night manager and asked him to come down and open it for me. I told him I was just going out for a walk because I couldn't sleep but the bundle I was carrying was a giveaway. I had a feeling that he would call the policemen who had brought me there the second I walked out.

I started down the road in the direction of the river towards a wooded area with only a few houses. Once I got on the fields I realized the terrain was too muddy to walk through - I was sinking in the mud up to my ankles. It looked to me that the best to make it to the river was by trespassing through a private house's yard. I got back to the road and started heading towards the nearest house. As I got near a car went by on the street, forcing me to jump into a ditch and duck to keep the headlight beams from shining on me. I was getting paranoid, unsure if someone was already looking for me. I had no way of knowing if the manager of the hotel had called the police on me or not.

As I got near the spot where the police had picked me up earlier that day, I noticed a driveway with a small fence separating the house's yard from the St. John River. Next to the fence was a large log that served as a barrier marking the end of the driveway. I hurried up the driveway when I saw the lights of a car turning into the driveway and heading in my direction. I dove again and laid flat behind the log barrier, pressing my body tightly to the ground while trying not to breathe of twitch a muscle.

The headlights shone directly over me as the car pulled up to the house. I froze the moment I saw a big guy who looked like a lumberjack getting out of the car along with a lady, probably his wife. I thought there and then that was the end for me. The couple, however, didn't notice me and started towards the house while I lay down motionless. Both of them went inside the house and I soon heard the deadbolt being turned to lock the door. I laid there still for a long time, until I realized that those people weren't coming back out again.

It was time for me to jump over the fence and find a spot where to enter the water and cross the river. I had all my possessions bundled tight inside a nylon jacket that I had wrapped around my neck. I hadn't brought much with me, only my passport, some money, and a few family pictures. I walked along the river banks for a little longer until I got to about one hundred feet from the bridge. There was a full moon in the sky and the water in the river appeared to be as smooth as glass all the way across.

I also noticed that the river was much wider than it had appeared on the map, and that the water was freezing cold at touch. I started to have second thoughts, but I knew that I wasn't going to have another opportunity, or an easier way to cross the river.

I took off my shoes at the water's edge and left them there with the rest of the clothes that I was wearing because I knew that the water would feel much colder against my skin with wet clothes on - it was that time of the year when it should have started snowing already. I eased myself into the water and started swimming across the river, constantly telling myself to stay calm no matter what happened. After swimming for about fifty feet the freezing river water had already chilled me through to my bones, while a sudden current started dragging me down the river.

I almost panicked when I realized that I was helplessly at the mercy of the strong current. I went under the bridge, missing one of the pilings by inches and kept picking up speed as the river carried me downstream. I started swimming with the current but, trying to head in an angle toward the other shore. I struggled in the current for a long time and almost passed out from the cold water. The nylon jacket that I had tied around my neck was filled with air and helped keep my head afloat working as a life preserver - the only thing that kept me from drowning. I began to lose my strength as I fought the current for such a long time.

I noticed a stone wall at the edge of the USA side of the river and further down a metal step ladder affixed to it. I made an extra effort and barely made it to the ladder, locking my arm around it and climbing the steps up to the safety of the ground above.

I was freezing cold and shaking like a leaf, with my whole face, my ears, my hands and my feet numb from the bitter cold. I headed towards the bridge to ask for help from the guards knowing that that wasn't going to make much further than that in my current condition. I was so exhausted that I could hardly walk. I thought that if I gave myself up to the U.S. Border Patrol they wouldn't return me to Canada or to Cuba in virtue of the "unwritten law", that father Macho had told me existed.

When I approached the guards, my mouth was shaking, and my voice trembled so hard that I could hardly get a single word out. The men gave me a hot drink and a blanket to cover myself. Once I started to warm up and feel better I started to explain to them where I came from, what I've done and that I wanted political asylum in the United States. I also told them that I ultimately wanted to reach Miami, Florida so I could pursue my music carrier.

The man in charge of the border checkpoint brought me an old pair of very large shoes to wear - mine were still on the Canadian side of the river where I had left them. After a short while, he escorted me back to the Canadian side of the bridge. I couldn't understand why they had done this and why the Canadian government would accept me back into their custody. That's when I realized that the "unwritten law" that father Macho had told me about wasn't true at all.

***

Once I was back on Canadian soil, the Canadian officers didn't place me under arrest, but told me that I would have to return to the processing center in Halifax. Instead, I returned to the hotel room that I had already paid for in Saint. Stephens. It would be useless for me to return to Halifax. I realized that if was to succeed in making it into the United States I would have to give it another shot at crossing the border right there. I left the hotel in the morning and started walking on the street down the row of houses located by the river when I came to an old, abandoned factory. I explored the backside of the building and found that there was a railroad bridge next to the factory that spanned to the U.S. side.

Without giving it a second thought, I started walking on the bridge's railroad tracks and soon enough was back in U.S. territory, in a city called Calais in the state of Maine. I headed towards the center of the city looking for a bus terminal. After asking around, I found out that the buses picked up and dropped off the passengers at a funky old hotel in Calais. I walked inside the hotel and bought a bus ticket to New York.

I walked into a bar at the back of the hotel to have a beer while I waited for my bus to arrive. I wasn't there for even five minutes when a border patrol officer came over to me and asked me for my identification papers. I didn't know what to say to say so, on impulse, I told him I told him that was an Italian from New York, (Robert Lamm, from the group Chicago, wrote a song from this Italian from New York titled "Halifax from New York"), all while trying to fake an Italian accent in my speech and a using a few Italian words. He then pointed to my pocket were my passport was and so I handed him the Cuban passport. The officer arrested me right away and told me in Spanish that I would be sent back to Canada again. At nine o'clock that night the border patrol officers put on a bus to back to Saint Stephens, Canada.

An hour later, I was still hanging out by the Canada-U.S. bridge in Saint Stephens, leaning against the railing and staring over to the U.S side the when a group of Canadian guys walked by and then turned around to ask me if I was the guy who had swam across the river. I told them that it was me, and then they asked me if I wanted to cross again and get into the United States.

I told them that I would like that very much. I followed them to the street next to the same hotel where I had been staying, where we met with another young Canadian who owned a Peugeot. My newly made Canadian friends asked this guy to drive me across the border in his car along with them. He agreed.

I got into the car and sat in the back in between two of the guys and the other two sat next to the driver in the front seat. We drove across the border over the bridge where one the guards stationed waved us to halt. We stopped so that the officer on duty could see who was in the car. The boys told him that we were going into the U.S. to play billiards at a local hall. The guard seemed to know them and didn't take a second look inside the car or noticed me; he probably thought that I was one of them and let us go through.

My Canadian friends told me they would help me get on a bus to New York once I made it clear to them that New York City was where I wanted to go from there. One of the guys called the funky hotel for me to find out at what time the next bus was departing for New York. He was informed that there wouldn't be a bus to New York until two 2 o'clock in the morning. We decided to go together to the hall where we stayed shooting pool and talking all night long. My friends even won some money for me by betting on the games they played. Two of them who were brothers told me that they would stay with me until the bus for New York arrived and make sure that I got on all right.

At around eleven o'clock at night we finished playing our last game of billiards and the two brothers and I started walking toward the funky hotel where the busses picked-up and dropped. As we got near, we searched for a place to hide out of sight and wait for the bus to arrive. I would be using the same bus ticket that I had purchased earlier.

There was a dark alley in the back of the funky hotel where we found a parked trailer truck. The truck's door was unlocked and all three of us hid inside the cabin. We stayed there talking and trying to stay warm as we waited for my bus to arrive.

Shortly after two o'clock we noticed the bus headlamps as the bus turned in front of the hotel. We got out of the truck and walked to where the bus had stopped. We all got startled when we noticed a border patrol officer standing by the hotel's front door facing the bus that I was supposed to board. I waited a few minutes and when I saw the officer walking around the bus I said goodbye to my friends. I rushed inside the bus without him seeing me and ran all the way to the back. There, I dove into the very last seat and laid down so that he couldn't see me through the window. I stayed down until the bus started off just hoping and praying that the officer had not spotted me getting on the bus.

I started my journey for New York City, determined to eventually make it all the way to Miami as I had originally planned. For the first three hours of that long trip I felt very apprehensive and feared being spotted at every stop that the bus made. However, the further we got from Canada, the safer I felt. Many hours later, the bus finally rolled into New York Port Authority bus station.

The red mark indicates the area where I crossed the border and swam to the United States from Saint Stephen to Calais.

From War to Rock 'n Roll

Part Three

Guillermo's life in the
United States

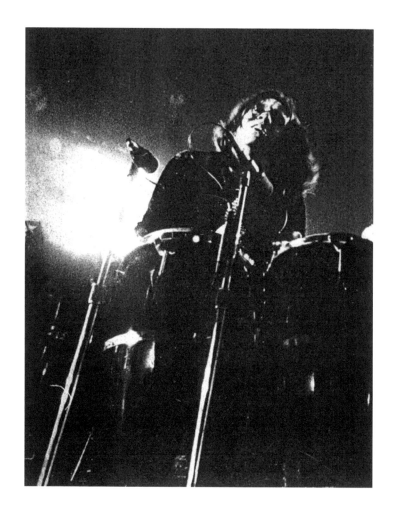

Guille Garcia Rodiles

From War to Rock 'n Roll

1.

My Arrival to the United States

The first people I ran into upon my arrival at the New York City bus station were two homosexuals who started blowing kisses at me. I felt very awkward and annoyed to be greeted in that fashion after all the trouble that I had gone through to get to the United States. It was not my idea of a welcoming reception.

I managed to communicate in Spanish with the woman at a help desk, who kindly gave me directions to the address of my step mother's parents, Ester and Mario, which I had brought from Cuba written in a piece of paper. Those were the first people that I had planned on visiting after arriving in the USA. The woman at the information center also explained to me how to dial the telephone number, and which bus would take me in the direction of the address I had with me. When I called the number, there was no answer, so I decided to get there by my own means.

The bus ride took about an hour, including crossing a bridge into the State of New Jersey. Once there, it didn't take me long to locate Ester and Mario's apartment. I remember the surprised look in their faces when they opened the door, they just couldn't believe that it was me, or had a clue how I had made it there. They were both very happy that I had arrived safely and totally amazed after to hear about my long odyssey.

By now, I was feeling very relived to at least be with family in the States, and at a safe place far away from Cuba. Mario and Ester were very nice people and offered me to stay with them. I happily accepted.

The next day, Ester and Mario brought me to the immigration center in New Jersey where I told the officers the story of how I

had made it from Cuba to the United States. After a long inter-
rogation, the U.S. immigration agents contacted the Canadian
immigration office in Halifax and requested my *dossier* to be sent
to their office in New Jersey. The immigration agents took my
picture and my fingerprints, and then said that I could not to
leave the State of New Jersey without their authorization. They
also gave me a document making me eligible for Social Security
benefits.

I spent the next few weeks at my relative's apartment. Mario
kept a violin and a mandolin, and we would play music and sing
Latin songs together almost every night until very late. We really
enjoyed being in each other's company. After a few weeks, I received the approval from the immigration office to travel around
the country at will, but I still had to inform them as of when I
would be leaving the state of New Jersey. I told them that I
wanted to go to Miami and my music career in that city. I gave
the immigration officers the address of my wife Christina father,
who lived in Miami. My plan was to bring Christina to the
United States and her father had offered me to stay with him until that time.

It was time for me to say goodbye to my kind hosts Ester and
Mario and get on a bus again, this time to Miami, Florida. After
a few hours on the bus we made a second stop in a small town in
Connecticut where a very pretty lady came on board. She walked
straight to the back and sat in the seat next to mine. I hadn't been
with any ladies for a long time and was pleased to have her as my
travel companion. My spoken English was very poor, but we had
a lot of fun trying to communicate mostly by using gestures and
sign language. I understood that she was on her way to Orlando,
Florida to visit some relatives and I told her where I had come
from and where I was headed to in Florida. Her name was Vicky.

The bus took an exit ramp and pulled up to a diner, so the
passengers could stretch their legs and have dinner. Vickie and I
went for a short walk on the bus and then sat together again. It

was obvious to me that the physical attraction was mutual and that she was very comfortable in my company. By then there were only a few people left on the bus besides Vickie and me. After the driver turned off the lights we became engaged in an intense romance. By morning, I felt much more relaxed. The bus trip with Vicky made me realize that I would not have any trouble relating to people from the United States, it was actually a lot easier than I had expected. Vickie and I traveled together until she got off in Orlando where we said goodbye. A few hours later, the bus finally arrived in Miami where I found Christina's father already waiting for me at the bus station. He told me that I could stay with him until I could get a place of my own.

Christina's father got me a job as a Volkswagen mechanic at a place called Bob Huston's Motors in Miami. I went to work the very next day to pay back the money that I owed Mario and Ester in New Jersey, and the money that Christina's father had sent me while I was in Canada. While working at the shop I ran into a friend from Cuba who introduced me to a guitar player, a young guy named Jesus. Jesus was trying to put a band together and he took me to the house of a friend of his who sold me a conga drum so that we could start rehearsing. We started to have rehearsals every afternoon.

In the band was Fermin, another Cuban who played bass, Raymond Casels on drums, Jesus and myself. We practiced very hard together for many months. I was still living with my father in law, who started to dislike me coming home late at night. I had been rehearsing with the band every day after work and then going to different clubs at night jamming with other bands. It upset me to be told when to come home and because he was starting to get down on me I knew that I would have to find my own place and move out soon.

Meanwhile, I was meeting a lot of musicians at different clubs in Miami and having a great time. With the money I had saved I bought a 1962 Chevy station wagon that eventually became my home after I left my father-in-law's house. I covered the back of the of the station wagon's windows with a coat of paint and put a mattress inside. I felt much better finally being on my own, out on the streets and free to do as I pleased.

One day at the shop, while I was pretty high on weed, I left the engine plug out when doing an oil change and watched in dismay the oil spilling all over the garage floor. The shop's foreman got very angry and yelled at me way more than was necessary, and then made me mop off all the oil from the floor. Some of mechanics who worked with me at the shop had been harassing me about my hair, which I had let grow quite long by then. That day I decided that I just didn't need the hassle and quit.

A few nights later, I was at a bar in Miami called *Evil People* when I ran into a Cuban guy named Marcos who was in the company of two young women. He asked me to join them at a party and afterwards we all stayed up until sunrise. Marcos was also living in the streets at the time.

The next day, Marcos told me he knew a way to get food easily since had little to no money. He showed me how he followed a catering truck that delivered trays of food to people's houses. When the delivery guy left the food trays by the doors, Marcos would run up to the house and grab them. For a while, I also procured my daily meals in this unorthodox fashion and managed not to go hungry.

One night, Marcos took me to a club called *The Climax* where I was introduced to the members of a band called Cracker, made up entirely of Cuban musicians. I started frequenting the *Climax* and jamming with this band, and soon we all got to be pretty good friends. Another band called *The Bird Watchers* was also playing regularly at the *Climax*. I learned they had been playing there for the past five years. A few months later, I started jamming with them also.

Those gigs with different bands in Miami went on for a few months and I eventually was asked to join a band called *Sylvester* and started playing all over the city with them - The Dream Lounge, The Cast Away and many others. That band broke up a year later because lack of work and we all went our separate ways. I joined another band called *Peace and Quiet*, which gave me my first experience at playing original music. I was now heading towards being part of a more professional band than any of the others I had played with before.

All the members of *Peace and Quiet* decided to move to Gainesville, Florida where we started playing in small clubs and shows all over northern Florida and Georgia. We didn't have a manager, so we had to become creative and book all the gigs ourselves. We had rented a small farm in Gainesville for the whole band to live in, which suited our purposes perfectly. The most significant gig I did with *Peace and Quiet* was at a show we did together with the *Chambers Brothers*. The band stayed together for two years and for no apparent reason everyone decided to break away and go on their own. Bobby, the bass player, and I returned to Miami to build a studio in his grandmother's garage with the idea of eventually putting another band together.

Bobby and I never fulfilled our dreams of getting another band together, we just lived for a while at his grandmother's house and played in the studio we had built. One night while I was in the Climax, I ran into a Cuban guy nicknamed *El Chaval* whom I knew from Havana. El Chaval offered to introduce me to Stephen Stills from *Crosby, Stills Nash and Young*, whom he was going to see to sell him some "recreational drug". I refused at first because I didn't want to have any kind of involvement selling drugs, but I realized this was a unique opportunity for me and decided to go along. Stephen Stills was staying at the time at a Holiday Inn in Coral Gables.

In hotel room, I found Stephen writing a Latin song called *Pensamiento* and he asked me for some advice on the prognostication and arrangement of certain lyrics. We started playing the song there, with Stephen playing guitar and me hitting the back of a guitar like a conga drum. Stephen asked me to stop by the next day at Criteria Studio in Miami where he was recording. It was 1972 and I had been in the United States for two years when I finally got my break into the real music world. I felt that I was on my way to getting somewhere.

At the recording studio, I played the congas for Stephen's album. That was the first time that I had ever played in a professional studio and was impressed with all the amazing equipment there. That day, I wrote a Spanish dialogue for the middle part of the song *Pensamiento*. We spent seven straight days in the studio working on that album. When that was done, all I wanted to do was to go to L.A.

Shortly thereafter, I made a road trip from Miami to Los Angeles with a girlfriend, Judie Swartz, in a brand-new Chevy Camaro and towing a van that was both my transportation and my home. Judy was the granddaughter of Casino mogul and mafia boss Mayer Lansky. The trip to L.A. was a very long drive but we got to see a lot of the country that way.

When we finally got to L.A., a friend of Judie's gave us a place to stay for the night and told us of a nice place at Santa Monica beach where we could park the van to live there for a while and not be bothered by the police. So, the next day we drove with the van to the beach and parked it there.

We started looking in the local newspapers and eventually found a cheap apartment that we could rent by the week and move in within a few days. I contacted the road manager for Stephen Stills, an Argentinean guy named Guillermo, who gave me some ideas of places to look for work. One of them was called Studio Instrument Rentals, and he also told me that Stephen would be finishing his album soon at Record Plant Studios in Los Angeles.

I went right away to Studio Instrument Rentals, SIR, and put up a card with my name and telephone number stating that I was a percussionist looking for work. A couple days later, I got a phone call from singer Claudia Lennear's manager, who asked me to come down to SIR and audition for her. The day after the audition, I received a call that I had been hired to play in Claudia's band, where Claudia doing the lead vocals. Charlie Grimes was playing lead guitar, Willie Weeks playing bass, Conrad Isador on drums, and myself in percussion.

I had been recording with this band for a month when I heard that Stephen Stills was finishing his album at Record Plant. One night, Claudia and I went to see him and we both ended up working for him on the same album that he hadn't been finished yet.

After New Year's Eve in 1973, Stephen invited me to his Colorado home for his birthday, which was on January 3rd. Stephen, Bobby Whitlock and I flew to Denver where I saw snow for the first time in my life. Right as we got off the plane, Stephen hit me with a snowball. I was very excited on this trip for I had been looking forward to the opportunity to see a real winter with snow and everything. However, I did notice right away that it was harder to breath in Denver because of the high altitude, something that didn't bother me too much. The wonderful scenery around me distracted me enough that I hardly noticed the effect of the altitude after a short while.

We drove from Denver to Boulder, where we picked up Stephen's car at Michael Jones's house, a house that was indeed the office for the band *Manassas*. From there, we drove to Stephen's house in Netherland, close to a ski resort called Eldora. Stephen's house was at 9,000 feet above sea level and it was incredibly beautiful. He had every imaginable instrument in the down stairs area and an enormous pool table. We stayed up all night and as soon as the sun came up we decided to go skiing which was to be a totally new experience for me.

As we walked out of the door in the morning, I noticed a mountain lion right in his backyard. In the daylight, the entire scenery around his house was overwhelming.

We drove from the house to the ski resort in what I thought

had to be the biggest snowmobile that was ever made. At the ski resort, we met with another percussionist named *Joe Lala* who had played in the album with us and had become a very good friend of mine. We would spend our time skiing during the day for that entire week, and then jam at Stephen's house at night. I learned to ski very quickly and got to love it.

One night while jamming at Stephen's house we had an interesting group of guests arriving at the front door. They were Jim Guercio, the producer of the band Chicago, and a guy named Hank, a keyboard player, Russ, the drummer and Al, the guitar player; all of them members of the rock-fusion band *Madura*. We ended jamming together for hours. That night, I was invited by the guys from *Madura* to stop by their place at the Caribou Ranch anytime I wanted. Stephen and I went down to the ranch several times to play with them, and also while they were performing at the Pioneer Inn in Netherland.

After a very nice vacation in Colorado I decided to return to Los Angeles. While in L.A., I got a call from Jim Guercio, who asked me to come over to Paramount Studios and do a recording session. When I got there, I realized that I was to play with a forty-piece orchestra. Guercio was producing the movie *Electra Glide in Blue*, and I would get to play for the soundtrack. There I was introduced to Terry Kath who was playing Bass, Jimmy Pankow, trombone, Lee Loughnane, trumpet and Walter Paraziader, saxophone - all members of the band Chicago. The conductor of the orchestra was Jimmie Haskell.

I was elated by having this incredible session with the largest group of well-known and talented musicians I had ever played with before - a dream coming true. We played all night in this wonderful studio and I got to know the guys of Chicago with whom I played music and got along with very well. Once the session was over I returned to my apartment on Crescent Heights.

Three days later, I got a phone call from the manager of a band called *Capitan Beyond* who offered me a job and asked me to travel with them to Macon, Georgia and record an album. I did not have a steady gig at the time, so I accepted the offer on the spot. First, we rehearsed for about one week at the instrument rentals studio in L.A., and then left for Macon, Georgia under contract with Capricorn Records.

When I woke up in Georgia the morning I learned there had been a snow storm overnight, the first one in more than twenty years. There were only two feet of snow but, the town of Macon was put under a state of emergency since they didn't have the equipment to deal with the snow. The entire city was paralyzed.

I had been recording for a few days with *Captain Beyond* when we decided that our drummer didn't really fit in with the band. I got on the phone and called Marty Rodriguez, a drummer friend of mine from Florida, and flew him up for an audition. Everyone in the band got to like Marty and he was in. The album started flowing nicely right away. In the band was Rhino, guitarist, Lee Dorman, bass - both formerly from Iron Butterfly, Rod Evans, a former lead singer for Deep Purple, Rusty Wynn, keyboard, Marty Rodriguez, drummer, and myself as a percussionist. After a month working in Georgia, we flew to San Francisco to finish the album at Record Plant. The album was called Sufficiently Breathless.

Captain Beyond album cover.

Captain Beyond
Sufficiently Breathless

During the 12 months since the release of Captain Beyond's much-acclaimed debut album, the former celestial rock & roll power quartet has greatly evolved.

Space Latin-Rock

They are now a sextet of more diversified, Latin-flavored proficiency, and their refreshed method of attack is more than well-represented by Captain Beyond's newest effort, *Sufficiently Breathless*. "We like to call Captain Beyond's new sound 'space Latin-rock,'" explains drummer and new member Marty Rodriguez. "There's a unique fusion of the two styles within the band now, and it feels great." Self-produced, *Sufficiently Breathless* was completed in the relaxed confines of the Record Plant in Sausalito after the basic tracks had been laid down at Macon's Capricorn Sound Studios.

Timbales Ace

The direction towards new ground began several months ago with the addition of timbales and conga ace Guille Garcia. An overwhelmingly successful attempt at supplementing Captain Beyond's percussion section, vocalist Rod Evans and lead guitarist Rhino had decided that the group was long-overdue for some spirited Latin-rhythms. "I was playing around Miami," Guille recalls his early days, "in a lot of Latin-soul groups and doing sessions here and there for people like Stephen Stills and Stevie Wonder. That was before I came out to LA as part of Claudia Lennear's band and met everyone in Captain Beyond. I had always wanted to be in a group I felt a part of and not just a back-up musician. So when they asked me if I wanted to join this band, I said I would because I knew it would be

just that. A *band*."

Up From Miami

Prior to the date Captain Beyond was to begin work on *Sufficiently Breathless*, drummer Bobby Caldwell, an original member, amicably parted company with the band, Says Rhino, "We had to take time out apart from each other." A hasty replacement with an English drummer named Brian (they can't recall his last name) proved inadequate when his services fell far short of meeting Captain Beyond's exacting studio recording standards. Guille wasted no time in calling up from Miami his fellow drummer and buddy nonetheless, Marty Rodriguez. Needless to say, Marty's style meshed perfectly with his fellow group-members and *Sufficiently Breathless* began its production.

Keyboard Crony

The third new Captain Beyonder is pianist Reese Wynans, formerly part of Boz Scaggs' group and the East-coast based Pandemonium. A good friend of Rhino's, when Reese heard that the band was cutting tracks in Macon, he visited the studios as a crony and ended up part of the group. Reese couldn't be more happy and content. "While I was there," Reese remembers, "they asked me to play keyboards on one song and it worked out well. I went back to my home in Sarasota and they called me to ask if I would finish the LP with them. We all liked the way it turned out, so here I am. I'm glad to be a part of the band."

Side One
1. SUFFICIENTLY BREATHLE
2. BRIGHT BLUE TANGO 4:1
3. DRIFTING IN SPACE 3:13
4. EVIL MEN 4:57

Side Two
1. STARGLOW ENERGY 5:1
2. DISTANT SUN 4:41
3. VOYAGES OF PAST TRAVELLERS 1:30
4. EVERYTHING'S A CIRCLE

All songs by Lee Dorman
PRODUCED BY CAPTAIN BEYOND

CAPTAIN BEYOND
SUFFICIENTLY BREATHLESS

Includes: Bright Blue Tango
Evil Men / Starglow Energy / Everything's a Circl

This album is also available and cassette. Captain Beyon other album on Capricorn F *Captain Beyond* (CP 0105).

CAPRICORN RECORDS

Write outs about Captain Beyond.

Captain Beyond band members.

After finishing the album, we all went back to L.A. but the band fell apart a few weeks later, mostly because of hard drug abuse and personality clashes.

After Captain Beyond broke up, I found myself back on the streets and with no idea of what to do next. That's when I got a call from Robert Lamm, the keyboard player for Chicago, who wanted me to do some percussion for his solo album which he had already started recording. I was supposed to vacate my apartment the next day, so I contacted Charlie Grimes of Claudia Lanier's band and asked him if I could store some things in a house that he was renting in Eagle Rock and offered him some cash. He told me that he was moving to San Francisco and that I could take over that house, so I ended up buying that house. Within a few days, Robert Lamm and I flew on Chicago's privet Jet out to Colorado to the studio on the Caribou Ranch where I was to overdub on his album.

Bobby had brought Russ from *Madura* playing drums for him, Terry Kath playing bass, Bobby playing all the keyboards and myself doing all the percussions. Other performers from the Beach Boys, the Pointer Sisters, and others also had a part in his album. At the same time, *Chicago's* seventh album was being recorded and I was also asked to play on it. This became one of my greatest personal successes in my music carrier, being asked to record and play with one of the greatest bands in the world. After both albums were finished, I was asked by Chicago to join them for an American tour.

Playing Congas with Chicago on stage.

Gold Record award with Chicago.

Playing Congas with Chicago in concert.

Gold Record Award with Joe Walsh

***

Soon after that tour ended I got my USA resident card and Chicago asked me to join them on a European tour. This European tour turned out to be a little complicated at the start because I left believing that I could enter every country with only my reentry permit but instead I found myself hassling at every embassy and consulate to get a visa to enter every country where the band was scheduled to play at.

After touring Europe with great success for thirteen days, we came back to the States and soon enough left for another American tour. Unfortunately, I fell in very bad health during this entire tour. By the time we were finished, I was very sick and told the band that was it for me. *Chicago* had to hire another percussionist to help me out. The time had come for me to take a break from the fast lane. The touring and the big band lifestyle had managed to run me down.

On stage with Chicago playing the congas.

Again, on stage with Chicago playing the congas.

Before boarding Chicago's private jet on our way to the Europen Tour.

After arriving in LA with Chicago from a concert tour

In the dressing room with Chicago.

Traveling on the private jet with the band Chicago.

Chicago 7th album

Left to Right: Lee, Terry, Peter, Guille, Danny, and Walter

Left to right: Walter, me, and Terry

```
THREE - CHICAGO

THURSDAY 13 SEPTEMBER

Freight leaves for England via British Air Ferries at 4 a.m.

Chicago
Luftansa 058
Departs Cologne    :   12:20 p.m.
Arrives London     :    1:45 p.m.

Accommodation - 13/14/15 September

Royal Garden Hotel
Kensington High Street
London W.8.4PT
01-937-8000.   Cable: ROYGARTEL.

Engagement - 13 September

Rainbow Theatre, London.
--------------------------------------------------

FRIDAY 14 SEPTEMBER

Rainbow Theatre, London.
--------------------------------------------------

SATURDAY 15 SEPTEMBER

Rainbow Theatre, London.
--------------------------------------------------

SUNDAY 16 SEPTEMBER

Freight leaves at 10 a.m. on British Air Ferry.

Chicago
BEA 014
Departs London    :   12:00 noon
Arrives Paris     :    1:00 p.m.

Accommodation - 16 September

Hotel Meurice
228 Rue de Rivoli
Paris 1,
Phone: 073-3240.  Cable: MEURISOTEL.

Engagement - 16 September

Palais de Sports, Paris.
--------------------------------------------------
```

European Tour Itinerary with Chicago

```
CHICAGO - EUROPEAN TOUR
WEDNESDAY 5 SEPTEMBER

Lufthansa 451
Departs L.A.      :  9:45 p.m.
Arrives Amsterdam:  4:25 p.m. 6 September

Accommodation - 6 & 7 September

Pulitzer Hotel
315-331 Prinsengracht
Amsterdam, The Netherlands.
Phone: (020) 22-83-33  Cable: PULITZER AMSTERDAM.
```

```
FRIDAY 7 SEPTEMBER

Concert - Concert-Gebouw, Amsterdam.
```

```
SATURDAY 8 SEPTEMBER

Bus from Amsterdam to Bremen.

Accommodation - 8 September

Park Hotel
IM Burgerpark 28
Bremen.
Phone: 0421-3400/31  Cable: PARKHOTEL.

Engagement - 8 September

(Racetrack) Bremen.
```

```
SUNDAY 9 SEPTEMBER

International TEE train
Depart Bremen   :  8:14 a.m.
Arrive Mannheim :  1:21 p.m.

Accommodation - 9 September

Steigenberger-Mannheimer Hof
Augusta Anlage 4-8
Mannheim.
Phone: 0621-45021  Cable: MANNHEIMHOF.
Engagement - 9 September

Ebert-Halle, Ludwigshaven.
```

European Tour Itinerary with Chicago

From War to Rock 'n Roll

***

After leaving *Chicago*, I focused on doing session work for groups like, *REO Speedwagon*, the *Hollywood Stars*, Bill Wayman, the bass player for the *Rolling Stones* on his two solo albums, Leon Russell, Stevie Wonder, Ray Manzarick, former Keyboard player for the Doors, etc. One night in the Record Plant in L.A. a big jam session was happening in a new studio that had just been built there. I was asked to join a great group of musicians including John Lennon, Ringo Star, Jimmy Smith, and others. This was a party as well as a jam, and everyone was having a great time. Joe Vitale, the drummer for Joe Walsh at the time, was there and told me he was rehearsing at S.I.R with Joe Walsh and *Barnstorm.*

The next day, Joe Vitale and I ran into each other in S.I.R told me that they were breaking in a new bass player, Brain Garofalo. Joe Walsh asked me to join the band that same night. He wanted me to play congas, timbales, and to switch in drums with Joe Vitale in certain songs in which Vitale could play piano and the timpani. I thought it was great that I was also going to play drums. This was the first time ever that I played drums professionally. We rehearsed for about a week and then went on to do a few American tours.

During my first tour with Joe Walsh and *Barnstorm* we recorded the "So What" album at Record Plant in New York. This was the second gold album I played on and had credit for during my music career in the United States.

By then, I had been in the United States for almost six years and I was extremely satisfied with my accomplishments as a musician. Soon thereafter, I started doing my own recordings with the expectations of someday making a great album of my own. My biggest dream was to see Cuba free again and go back to bring peace and music for all my people.

Bill Wayman, Bass player for the Rolling Stones and
Guille Garcia Rodiles.

Joe Walsh and me.

With Joe Walsh and Barnstorm

2035 WESTWOOD BOULEVARD, LOS ANGELES, CALIFORNIA 90025 / (213) 474-1507 • TELEX #677537

ITINERARY FOR JOE WALSH & BARNSTORM

DAY	DATE	CITY	HOTEL	SHOWS
MON.	JUNE 3	LITTLE ROCK	CAMELOT INN	0
TUES.	JUNE 4	LITTLE ROCK	CAMELOT INN	0
WED.	JUNE 5	LITTLE ROCK	CAMELOT INN	0
THURS.	JUNE 6	LITTLE ROCK	CAMELOT INN	1
FRI.	JUNE 7	NEW ORLEANS	MARIE ANTOINETTE HOTEL	1
SAT.	JUNE 8	MOBILE	HOLIDAY INN-DOWNTOWN	1
SUN.	JUNE 9	MOBILE	HOLIDAY INN-DOWNTOWN	0
MON.	JUNE 10	LAKE CHARLES	DOWNTOWNER MOTOR INN	0
TUES.	JUNE 11	LAKE CHARLES	DOWNTOWNER MOTOR INN	1
WED.	JUNE 12	CORPUS CHRISTY	SHERATON MARINA INN	1
THURS.	JUNE 13	SAN ANTONIO	HILTON PALACIO DEL RIO	0
FRI.	JUNE 14	SAN ANTONIO	HILTON PALACIO DEL RIO	1
SAT.	JUNE 15	SHREVEPORT	SHERATON INN	1
SUN.	JUNE 16	HOUSTON	WHITEHALL	1
MON.	JUNE 17	AUSTIN	TERRACE MOTOR INN	1
TUES.	JUNE 18	WICHITA	HOLIDAY INN-PLAZA	0
WED.	JUNE 19	WICHITA	HOLIDAY INN-PLAZA	1
THURS.	JUNE 20	TULSA	HOLIDAY INN DOWNTOWN	1
FRI.	JUNE 21	OKLAHOMA CITY	HILTON INN	1
SAT.	JUNE 22	CLEVELAND	SHERATON INN	0
SUN.	JUNE 23	CLEVELAND	SHERATON INN	1
MON.	JUNE 24	HOME		

American Concert Tour Itinerary with
Joe Walsh and Barnstorm

From War to Rock 'n Roll

This book ends here but my story continues with my huge
musical family on http://youtube.com/rodiles1147

The Rodiles family, Miami, 2017